Marketing Your Educational Leadership Skills

How to Land the Job You Want

John C. Daresh

A SCARECROWEDUCATION BOOK

The Scarecrow Press, Inc.
Lanham, Maryland, and London
2002

A SCARECROWEDUCATION BOOK

Published in the United States of America
by Scarecrow Press, Inc.
A Member of the Rowman & Littlefield Publishing Group
4720 Boston Way, Lanham, Maryland 20706
www.scarecroweducation.com

4 Pleydell Gardens, Folkestone
Kent CT20 2DN, England

British Library Cataloguing in Publication Information Available

Library of Congress Cataloging-in-Publication Data

Daresh, John C.
   Marketing your educational leadership skills : how to land the job you want / John C. Daresh.
      p. cm.
   "A Scarecrow education book."
   Includes bibliographical references and index.
   ISBN 0-8108-4266-1 (pbk. : alk. paper)
      1. School administrators. 2. School management and organization—Vocational
guidance. 3. Educational leadership. I. Title.

   LB2831.8 .D37 2002
   371.2'0023—dc21
                                                                                    2002018725

Contents

Acknowledgments

This book was written to help people who have the potential of providing strong, visionary leadership to schools find the right jobs so that they can invest their talents in helping students learn and grow. If this opening sentence sounds like a description of you, it may be because you have had the opportunity to learn from other "strong, visionary leaders" who have helped students. It is because of a desire to ensure a continuing supply of effective educational administrators that this book has been written.

Fortunately, there are many role models around who give witness to the fact that the goals of this book can actually be achieved in the future. Among those leaders who have helped inspire me and give me confidence that we will continue to have success in our schools are many of my colleagues with whom I have worked in Texas, Colorado, and Ohio. Included are many who deserve particular respect and mention here: Nick Cobos, Jim Kelch, Mary Lou Martinez, Debbie Patin, Charlie Vass, Don Schulte, Jim Hess, and Ed Ginty are but a few who immediately come to mind. I also owe a debt of gratitude to other colleagues with whom I have worked in higher education. A few who quickly surface as role models and contributors to my effectiveness are Jim LaPlant, Bruce Barnett, Gene Hall, Rodolfo Rincones, Karen Dunlap, Myrna Gantner, and Ron Capasso.

I also wish to acknowledge the friendship and support of Tom Koerner, my colleague for many years when he served the National Association of Secondary Schools, who now continues his service to education as an editor at Scarecrow Education.

Finally, most sincere thanks go to my family. I thank my wife, Stephanie, and daughter, Bridget, for all of their support in this writing effort and so many other projects. Their adventures as a school staff member and as a student in public schools for the past few years have given me many insights that are contained in these pages. For Bridget: in just a few short years, you are going to be contributing in schools as the teacher you have dreamed of becoming for so many years. You will be able to market the skills and vision that have held since starting school in Greeley and soon graduating from high school in El Paso.

Introduction

Belinda Thomas was just about finished with all of the coursework and other requirements needed to get Mideastern University's final endorsement of her application for a state principal's certificate. She had a master's degree in music education but had wanted since her third or fourth year of teaching to become a principal. So, she had been working part-time for nearly three years to complete the educational administration courses that would qualify her for the principal's license. She knew that she would probably need to serve as an assistant principal for a few years, but after that, she wanted to achieve her goal of becoming an elementary school principal.

As Belinda was driving to Mideastern to take the final exam in her last required course, a thought came across her mind. She had invested so much time and energy in completing the required courses, tests, assessments, and internships that she had not given a lot of thought to the practical side of actually seeking and eventually landing an administrative job. In all the books she had read about supervision, school law, finance, and all the other things she had studied, no professor or class had really touched on the one thing she now desperately wanted to consider: how to get a job as a school administrator.

Belinda is no different from the thousands of other students each year who actively pursue careers in the field of educational administration. Their preparation focuses almost exclusively on acquiring information *about* administration and management. Theoretical knowledge is stressed as the primary content of most preservice programs. In many cases, that focus is augmented by trying to assist people in learning techniques related to *how* to administer. This is normally done through increased attention to such activities as planned field experiences, internships, or other efforts to place aspiring administrators out in the field to learn at the sides of practicing school leaders.

In recent years, research identifying instructional leadership as a key ingredient in effective schools has caused attention to be directed increasingly at the ways in which future school administrators are being prepared. As a consequence, many universities have worked to develop administrator preparation programs that will enable individuals to face the challenges that await them when they step into the principalship or some other administrative role. One recent concerted effort to improve preservice programs was through the work of the Danforth Foundation (one of the largest philanthropic organizations in the United States) in the late 1980s and early 1990s. As a result of that work and other approaches launched over the past decade, efforts have been made to improve curriculum, instructional practices, and the ways in which university programs may be enhanced through better relations with practitioners in the field. In short, there has been a general recognition that traditional strategies designed to prepare future principals did not work, but changes have been made, and more improvement will likely be made in the future.

Despite these efforts, however, a final ingredient has been missing from the majority of preservice programs. That ingredient—how to help people find the job for which they have been prepared—is the focus of this book. The assumption is made in this book that you have participated in (or you are now participating in) a preservice preparation program and that the program has provided you with basic knowledge and skills needed to do your job as an assistant principal, principal, or some other school administrator. But now, you need some advice in getting that first position. Like Belinda Thomas, you are all set to begin, but you may need a few tips to get you going. You might also currently be a practicing school administrator who is now interested in looking for a new job; if so, the material in this book may be quite helpful to you as well.

In all probability, you are qualified for and capable of assuming a leadership position in a school. However, you may be ignored during the selection and hiring process, largely because you may not have a complete understanding of what it takes to achieve some important career goals. In terms borrowed loosely from the private sector, you may be a person who has a lot of talent—a "good product"—but despite this, you do not seem to be able to "close the deal" and get the job you want. What you need to do is learn an approach to marketing your product, and your product is nothing less than your ability to provide effective leadership to a school.

A MARKETING MODEL

In order to help you in selling your valuable product of effective educational leadership, the chapters of this book will be devoted to the presentation of a model designed to help you in marketing and selling your talent. This Marketing Model consists of six steps:

1. Knowing the product
2. Knowing the customer
3. Choosing the target audience
4. "Lining up your ducks"
5. Presenting yourself: résumés, portfolios, and interviews
6. Reflecting on the process

These steps may appear to be closely linked with the marketing of private-sector goods and services. In fact, following the model presented here may also be appropriate for efforts to sell furniture or farm products or time-sharing programs in Florida. If this seems a bit out of line with your interest in trying to find a job as a school administrator, remember that, just as with furniture or time-sharing, you have a product to sell to potential buyers. The product is your talent, namely, the ability to lead a complex organization such as a school or school district. And always keep in mind that a school is not simply a building with children in it. Instead, a school is a representation of hopes, values, and dreams for an entire community. As a potential leader of that very important community resource, you will have some very distinct responsibilities to fulfill. Probably the most important are the following:

- Taking care of a multimillion-dollar physical plant and facility. Even if the school is not terribly modern or impressive to the eye, and even if it does not represent state-of-the-art planning and design, always remember that any school building is the best that a particular district can afford. And then remember that you will be the person who holds the key to that building.
- Representing the best interests and needs of dozens, if not hundreds, of adults each day.

- Taking care of hundreds, if not thousands, of students each day. Above all, this is truly the most powerful and important role that any school administrator will have. People to whom you are selling your leadership talent have a very definite right to expect that you will honor, respect, and serve the most important resource in their community—the children who attend your school. This is indeed an awesome responsibility, but it is the great challenge that you face when you tell the world that you are ready to lead a school.

Your buyers are parents, community members, professional educators, staff, school board members, and, of course, students. All of these groups have a vital interest in the quality of the school or district you propose to lead.

Marketing leadership talent in schools can be thought of as trying to sell other, more mundane products to clients. As a result, this book contains certain concepts and terms from private-sector marketing. At the same time, however, it is critical to realize that the stakes associated with selecting the right leader for a school go well beyond simply selecting the most comfortable new sofa or the seed corn with the greatest yield. This book will continually prod you to understand why having an effective leader is so vital to the well-being of a school, district, and community in general.

PLAN OF THE BOOK

The chapters of this book correspond to the steps of the Marketing Model presented previously. Each chapter begins with a brief scenario depicting the primary issue described in the chapter. The chapter content follows a pattern that asks you to respond actively to a number of different questions and challenges. These questions are designed to assist you in understanding the concepts and practices of the chapter. The ultimate goal of this book is to provide you with the confidence necessary to ensure that your efforts to find an appropriate leadership position in education will be rewarded.

There can be no absolute guarantee or promise that simply following the steps of the Marketing Model will always get you the job you want. There are, of course, many variables related to the selection of a principal, assistant principal, or superintendent. You may develop a brilliant and outstanding strategy to market your talents, only to find out that a person who appears much less qualified gets the job that you want. Chalk it up to politics, favoritism, unfairness, or anything else you may wish to call it, but not everyone who should get a job actually gets a job. And perhaps that will ultimately be one additional step in the Marketing Model: *be cool and patient*.

CHAPTER 1

Knowing the Product

Calvin Rossi was really frustrated. He had just opened a letter from the Upper Croute Valley Schools in which he was officially notified that the district had selected someone else to serve as the principal of their new middle school. Cal was not very surprised at the news. He had been through this process often enough to know that, when a letter came, it was always bad news. When a district offered you a position, they normally did so by phoning you first; rejection letters sent to finalists always came later, after the first choice had accepted the job. Cal had seen this pattern several times over the past two years as he had tried to leave his job as an assistant principal at Green Earth Middle School in the Mad City School District.

This rejection really bothered Cal. He had thought he had a chance to land this job at Upper Croute Valley. The last three or four interviews in other districts had been helpful to Cal because he began to understand what people on the interview teams wanted to hear from candidates. As a result, he had begun to get a sense of how to match his responses to the kinds of things that he thought the people in a particular school or district wanted to hear. For example, last month, he had applied for the principalship over at Clermont Heights, a small school serving a very wealthy neighborhood in the Kings Meadow Schools, a district known for parents who expected their children to be admitted to very prestigious colleges and universities. Cal had made every effort to change his expressed views on education to emphasize the importance of programs for gifted and talented students. He really didn't believe in them, but he knew that the best way to get an administrative job was by giving a community what it wanted. He had geared his responses to the selection committee at Upper Croute in the same way, but this time he had downplayed the gifted program and spoke more about his commitment to the needs of working-class students, as he had read that fewer than 30 percent of the parents in the district had attended college.

As Cal began to think back on his experiences, he realized that he wasn't getting any closer to getting that first principalship. As he began to think over the answers he would give for his next possible employment interview, he was very frustrated and again could not understand what was keeping him from his goal.

Calvin Rossi may be an excellent prospect for a principalship in a school district. The problem is, no one may ever really know that. Calvin may not come close to the point of being seriously considered for an administrative post, because if he were to send in a job application to most school districts, he would not look very different from most other people looking for work as a principal or assistant principal. Reviewers of applications would know that Mr. Rossi is male; has a certain number of years of prior work experience, probably mostly in education; has a bachelor's and a master's degree from accredited institutions; and has (or soon will have) completed all requirements for relevant teaching and administrative licenses.

With the exception of assumptions about the candidate's gender, legislation over the years has made it increasingly difficult to determine much about the personal characteristics of any job applicant. There is good reason for this, of course. People should not be hired simply because of their age, weight, gender, race, ethnicity, national origin, religious conviction, lifestyle, or sexual orientation. This legislation is an effort to ensure that the selection of candidates for teaching and administrative positions is well intentioned and is directed toward the principle of keeping job candidates on an even playing field. This is good policy, but it does not really help employers learn much more about individuals beyond "name, rank, and serial number" matters. And to some extent, applicants may be disadvantaged by this because they are not likely to be understood for their unique personalities and their ability to serve as outstanding teachers or leaders.

This is a perplexing dilemma. On the one hand, you do not wish to be subject to possible discriminatory hiring practices or to be hired not on your own merit but simply because you are connected to someone who knows someone who knows. . . . On the other hand, if you accept the metaphor presented in this book, namely that searching for and being selected for a leadership role in schools is similar to marketing a product in business, how will your uniqueness shine through?

Before anyone can be effective at marketing and selling, it is critical to know a good deal about the product being sold. A person with no knowledge of Fords or automobiles in general will not likely convince another to purchase a Thunderbird or a Mustang. The same is true of an individual who is trying to sell his or her services as a principal or assistant principal: before you start with the marketing of your educational leadership skills, you have to know the nature of what it is you want others to buy. Again, it is critical to appreciate the fact that very little information will be evident to potential customers if their knowledge of most job applicants is limited to simple statements of job qualifications presented on paper. But before you can successfully convince your buyers that you are better suited for a job than other candidates, you need to look carefully at yourself to appreciate your unique skills and qualities.

The technique recommended here for enabling you to get to "know the product" better is the development of a personal educational platform. This process, first suggested by Chris Argyris (1982) and later applied to education by Thomas Sergiovanni and Robert Starratt (1995) is promoted here as a key feature of administrators' professional development.

PLATFORMS AND THEIR DEVELOPMENT

Simply stated, a personal educational platform is a written statement of your most fundamental beliefs and values concerning issues of importance to you as a practicing or aspiring educational leader. As it is so personal, there is no prescription as to the perfect or best way to develop a platform statement, but several authors (Barnett, 1990; Kottkamp, 1982; Daresh, 2001) have recommended formats to follow in order to construct coherent statements of professional beliefs. You may wish to follow the model here that consists of little more than the writing of narrative, personal responses to the following questions:

1. What is my view of the purpose of schooling? Do we have schools primarily to train students for later success in the workplace? To promote self-actualization? To acquire fundamental or basic skills? Or is schooling largely an economic and political activity, in that a nation must have strong education to ensure its continuing role in a global economy? You may wish to write down some of your personal responses to this basic question now.

_____

_____

_____

_____

_____

2. What are some key ingredients of an adequate education for all students? Is adequacy defined by the acquisition of traditional basic skills of literacy and numeracy? If so, what do you think about the importance of learning about technology? Where do you stand on issues such as moral and ethical development of children? What about the importance of self-esteem? There are no absolutely correct ways to consider any of these choices, but based on your personal views of education and schooling, you may wish to identify some of your personal values in the following space.

_____

_____

_____

_____

_____

3. What is the appropriate role for students? Some educators believe that students learn only when they become actively involved in their own education (i.e., that learning will not take place in a setting that stresses reactive behavior). On the other hand, some educators argue that the fundamental activity of schooling is the transmission of knowledge and skills from someone who has these attributes (a teacher) to someone who does not (a student), and that therefore, the best learning occurs when students collect information from teachers. Reviewing responses to this issue also reveals a person's general perspective and assumptions related to students in general: Can students be trusted to assume an active role as learners? Or is a more controlling approach needed by teachers, administrators, and other educators because students cannot be "left alone?"

_____

_____

_____

_____

_____

4. What is the appropriate role for teachers? Again, how one answers this question may be a reflection of a larger and even more powerful set of values. Are teachers true professionals capable of making independent and informed decisions and choices that are in the best interest of students, colleagues, and their schools? Or, is the prevailing perception of teachers one of employees who work in schools, much like factory workers or others who toil largely to meet personal needs and interests? Are teachers replaceable units, or is each teacher a unique talent who is able to make significant contributions to schooling as a result of personal qualities and talent? Clearly, how you view the basic qualities of teachers has a great deal to do with how you as a school administrator are likely to define "appropriate" duties and responsibilities of the teachers in a school.

_____

_____

_____

_____

_____

5. What is the appropriate role for parents and other members of a school community? Some schools greet visitors with a sign or decal on the front door with a statement such as "This is your school—and welcome to it." But, do you feel that way? Are parents equal partners in the educational program, or do you see them as tolerated intruders? What about the many members of your local community who pay taxes but do not have children enrolled in your (or any other) school? The business community has made it clear that it has strong perceptions of what public schools ought to be doing. But what are your personal views regarding the business community and its involvement with schools?

_____

_____

_____

_____

_____

6. What is my personal definition of curriculum? Regardless of many recent movements across the nation to increase educational quality control through more rigorous oversight of school curriculum,

it remains a reality that curriculum is still largely defined by what an individual teacher wishes to focus on with his or her students. School administrators also affect this reality by choosing to enforce (or not enforce) external curriculum demands. Once again, such choices are largely matters of individual preferences and values. The fact is that, as an educational leader, you need to have a clear understanding of what the curriculum is and what it should be in a school where you work. For example, how inclusive should a school's curriculum be?

_____

_____

_____

_____

_____

7. What do I want the school to become? What is your personal vision for the school in which you now work, or for any school where you might serve as a leader? What kinds of hopes and dreams for a more effective school drive your work? What are your goals and ideals?

_____

_____

_____

_____

_____

8. How will I know if students have learned? The ultimate goal of any school (and every school leader) must be to ensure that learning has taken place among students. But what are the indicators, at least in your mind, of whether or not this has really taken place? Some would say that students' scores on standardized achievement tests are valid indicators, whereas some say that learning really occurs only when established outcomes or performance indicators are reached. What is your perspective on this issue?

_____

_____

_____

_____

_____

9. How do I want others to see me? Do you want to be thought of as a person with enough expertise to respond effectively to all questions? Do you wish to be known as a great teacher of teachers? How about serving as a mediator in all types of conflict and dispute? Remember that others will often see you as you wish to be seen, whether your wishes are on a conscious level or not. Therefore, it is important to reflect on the kinds of images that you wish to project. How do you hope to be viewed by your teachers, students, staff, parents, and community members? Think about this issue on two levels: First, what would others say about you as a person? Second, what image would you hope to project as a principal or school leader?

---

10. What are my nonnegotiable values? This last question is the single most important one to be addressed in any platform statement. Ultimately, this question asks you to consider the kinds of values that, if violated by the school system or by other people with whom you must work, would cause you to "throw your keys on the table" and seek employment elsewhere.

WHAT DO YOU DO WITH YOUR PLATFORM?

The value of a personal educational platform is not in simply writing it out one time, putting it in a file cabinet, and then letting it sit for the remainder of your professional career. Rather, it should be seen as a living document or statement regarding the boundaries that you are willing to put around different decisions made during your career. Platforms will change as you move through your professional life. For example, your thinking about the desirability of standardized testing as a way to measure student growth and progress may change drastically between today and some point in your future. Your thinking is always a "work in progress." Your vision of perfect teachers or ideal students may be modified greatly as you move further away from the days when you were a teacher or when you interacted daily with students in a classroom. A platform is never meant to be a document set in stone. Rather, it is important that you review your platform periodically and make changes as you alter your views and attitudes as a professional educator.

Developing a formal statement of personal values through the preparation of an educational platform has many important applications that can assist you in your career as an educational leader. For one thing, developing clarity regarding your nonnegotiable values—even though these might change in the future—can be a genuine help to you as you think about making changes in jobs, moving to other school systems, accepting transfers within the district, and so forth. For example, there are some excellent school leaders who have turned their backs on what others might have thought were "perfect" jobs because, in their minds, taking these positions would cause them to compromise their important professional values.

Second, a clear statement of your platform is of value to those with whom you are to work, both at your individual school site and outside it. No one advocates printing multiple copies of your platform and then sending them around to everyone you might meet (or nailing a copy to the cathedral door!). However, there are people who have taken the time to write their platforms from time to time and who now have a stronger grasp of their own values, so that those around them can see what "makes them tick." This not only has the benefit of enabling principals to be open to their staffs, but it is also a powerful way to model communication skills that lead to a more effective school in general.

Finally, the ultimate value of developing a clear statement of your educational platform may be that it can serve as the foundation for long-term personal professional development. Too often, educators simply drift through their careers, engaging in periodic and sporadic attempts to find programs of professional growth and development. These are often based largely on trying to learn more about one hot topic or another or are undertaken because the central office has made it clear that all principals ought to jump on a certain bandwagon. In many cases, principals simply respond to the visions or platforms of others. It would be far more effective and desirable for principals to engage in systematic career planning that is rooted in their own values and sense of where they believe they are going or what is truly important to them. Therefore, it is strongly suggested that you begin your professional development portfolio with a clear statement of your platform, so that other elements of your portfolio can flow in a logical sequence from this strong foundation. In appendix A, you will find some excerpts from platforms developed by school administrators around the country. These may help you in developing your statement.

YOUR PERSONAL PLAN

In the next few pages, you may wish to begin sketching out some of the more critical elements of your own educational platform. This can be used as a way to guide the development of your entire professional portfolio, as described later in this book. You may wish to consult, and respond to, the questions posed earlier in this chapter, or you may prefer to respond to other critical issues of your own choosing that will provide an even greater sense of who you are as a professional educator. In this way, you may be in a better place than Calvin Rossi, the disappointed applicant who was described in the opening scenario. Cal spent so much time trying to come up with answers that would satisfy others that he never let people really know who he was.

_____

_____

_____

_____

_____

Now that you have written the "planks" of your platform, the last step in this process involves a clear statement of what you plan to do to implement your personal vision of effective practice. Once you have completed this last step, share your statements with one or two close friends, family members, or colleagues with a simple request for them to indicate whether or not they recognize you in the words on the paper. If they don't, you may wish to reconsider some of what you have written and decide whether or not you have written a true description of what you believe.

_____

_____

_____

_____

_____

In the final analysis of this step in the Marketing Model, you might wish to return to the purpose behind the platform exercise. As you consider your platform statement, remember that the "real" issues likely to be on the minds of those who are reviewing you as an applicant might be questions such as these:

1. What makes you so special and unique that you are better than any other person seeking this position?
2. Under what circumstances would you consider withdrawing your name from consideration for this position?
3. What might make you resign from this or any other position?
4. What makes this position so special for a person with your capabilities, experiences, and values?

A FEW FINAL THOUGHTS

Although the development of a personal educational platform is a very important exercise to follow, a few words of caution are necessary. If all that the platform becomes is a written statement of some ideas that you hold to be desirable, it will not be of any long-term and practical value in your career development. Simply writing out a description of what you think others would like to hear from a job applicant is an empty exercise. Instead, make certain that whatever you say can be matched in reality by actual practice. In short, do you "walk your talk"? If a person who knew you well were to read your platform statement, would he or she immediately recognize you in the words? If not, you may be putting out some kind of "false advertisement." Remember that whatever you claim as a belief or value will be tested many times as you step into a leadership role in schools. And that is something that you need to keep in mind as you even consider applying for a job in some settings. If you really believe what you state in your educational platform, are there some schools where you would not be comfortable working—regardless of how much they might pay, where the schools are located, or what other benefits might be present? Remember that, in the long run, you are not likely to be very effective in a place that does not "fit." Ultimately, that may be the most important thing that you can learn by taking the time to prepare a platform statement.

Also, no platform stays the same for an entire lifetime. Circumstances in your life will change and will in turn change the ways in which you look at a variety of issues. First-year teachers look at some things quite differently than those who have been "in the trenches" for ten or more years. Assistant principals are likely to have different perceptions than principals. Becoming a parent changes some of a teacher's perceptions regarding children as students. Remember that a good platform is a living document that will likely change as you proceed through life. Revisit your statement periodically to see if it is still a reasonable representation of who you are, or at least of who you want to be.

CHAPTER SUMMARY

This chapter presented the importance of knowing your personal values as a first, critical step in being able to market yourself effectively as a school leader. Just as the fundamental characteristics of any product that is to be sold to consumers must be clearly displayed, when the "product" being marketed is you, then you must make it clear what makes you a potential candidate for a position.

The strategy suggested as a way to engage in a thoughtful review of your most essential beliefs and characteristics is the preparation of a personal educational platform. There are many different ways to carry out this activity; one approach is suggested in this chapter. The values to be included in the platform were identified, both from the perspective of a school or district that would need to know more about you as a potential leader and also from your point of view as an applicant for a job. The whole idea with any selection process is to match the right person with the right job, and developing a platform can be a most effective way to guide this practice.

BIBLIOGRAPHY

Argyris, Chris (1982). *Reasoning, learning, and action: Individual and organizational.* San Francisco: Jossey-Bass.

Barnett, Bruce (1990). Using alternative assessment measures in educational leadership programs: Educational platforms and portfolios. *Journal of Personnel Evaluation, 6,* 141–151.

Daresh, John (2001). *Beginning the principalship: A practical guide for new school leaders.* Thousand Oaks, CA: Corwin Press.

Kottkamp, Robert (1982). The administrative platform in administrative preparation. *Planning and Changing, 13,* 82–92.

Sergiovanni, Thomas, and Robert Starratt (1995). *Supervision.* (5th ed.). New York: McGraw-Hill.

CHAPTER 2

Knowing the Customer

Alicia Dillsworth drove to the interview at Banbury North Elementary School with more confidence than she had had at any places where she had applied for a principal's position during the past year. Although the school was located in a community about three hours away from her home in South Warwick, she felt well prepared for today. She had never been to this town before, but she had called a few friends who lived near there, and she had checked Banbury North's records on the state education department's Web site. She had noted that the school had a diverse student population that included students of Hispanic, African American, Native American, Asian, and Anglo descents. Though the school had never achieved the state department's highest award for scores achieved on the annual statewide standardized student achievement test, she had noted that there had been a slow but steady increase in student scores for the past three years. She was sure that one of the selling points for the interview committee would be her promise that, as their new principal, she could get Banbury North "over the top" within the next two years.

She really wanted this job, which would be her first principalship. She had even checked out the Web site for the local community newspaper on two or three occasions since she had noticed the opening at Banbury North. She had paid particular attention to the "Letters to the Editor" section and had noticed that most contributors appeared to favor rather traditional, conservative causes such as opposing gun control, lowering taxes, and supporting family values. There were even a few people who wanted the local school board and superintendent to adopt the controversial practice of requiring a "moment of spiritual renewal" after the reciting of the Pledge of Allegiance in all district schools, to begin the school day. Alicia had no problem with any of this, as she had always favored more conservative values herself, a fact reinforced when she recently reread her educational platform.

Alicia had paid attention to a lot of small details when researching this job. She had noticed that the local newspaper carried advertisements for stores that were located in the local shopping mall, but the stores tended to carry merchandise in the lower price ranges. There were none of the high-end or upscale boutiques that she enjoyed visiting in her present community. Alicia preferred to dress more stylishly for work, but she had made certain that the outfit she selected for today's interview was not too trendy. She had made certain that no designer labels were visible on her clothing.

When she finally arrived at the school, she was careful to follow proper protocol by making certain that she was there ahead of her appointed time. She also made certain that she did not park in any reserved parking places in the lot in front of the school. Although she knew the room number assigned for her interview, she checked in at the main office as directed by the sign conspicuously posted on the front door of the school. She was friendly but not too chatty with the office staff members who greeted her. After all, she wanted to be the principal of this school in a few months, and she knew that she might not always be able to be best friends with everyone who worked there.

When it was time for Alicia's interview, she was asked to follow one of the selection committee members down the hall to where she would meet the committee. Suddenly, she noticed that her plans did not seem to match the scene before her. Instead of the group she thought she would see in what she had believed to be a diverse, middle-class, conservative community, she noticed that the parents were extremely well dressed and that nearly all were Japanese. Two introduced themselves as doctors, and she recognized one of them as having recently been on television for an interview about employee motivation in Japan. The teachers, who made up more than half of the interview committee, sat noticeably well away from the community members. They were quite reserved, and they seemed to dress more in the same way as Alicia usually did. All the teachers were Anglo.

What Alicia had failed to do in her planning for the day was to visit the community in person or to read the newspapers more carefully. If she had, she might have noticed the fact that a large new regional production plant for a Japanese auto company had just been placed in this town. It had been a real coup for the community, which was now adjusting to many very new residents—both in terms of language and ethnicity, and also in terms of lifestyles, economic backgrounds, and education levels. And Banbury North served a new housing development where the majority of the plant's senior management team from Japan had chosen to buy their homes.

Alicia left the interview quite confused and not at all confident about her presentation. She had worked hard to prepare for this by getting to know the community, but now she was certain that all her planning would be of no value because she had made a grave error in understanding the nature of her new school's community.

Selling any product requires a person to do a kind of marketing analysis of potential buyers. For example, it is not likely a very successful plan for a high-end luxury car dealer to open a showroom in a lower-middle-class working community where most residents could not afford a Lexus, Cadillac, BMW, or Jaguar. Or, in some cases, the prevailing culture may be one in which local residents are more likely to invest money in fashionable trucks rather than in automobiles of any type. Good and effective companies do their homework and know their probable customers before they invest in a sales effort. Consider the McDonald's hamburger restaurant chain, which never allows one of its stores to be built in a location where there are not enough possible passersby who may stop in for a fast meal.

The same considerations are necessary when a person is trying to land a job as a school administrator in a particular community. As Alicia knew when she was getting ready for her interview, some schools are located in very conservative communities, but others are found in places where innovative practices are the expectation of parents and other local patrons. Some schools serve communities where nearly all children go to private universities, but others are found in places where most high school graduates go to work immediately in local industries after graduation. In addition, as Alicia discovered in this chapter's opening scenario, there are also some communities that change, often quite rapidly and without much warning. Perhaps a community's residents were wealthy a few years ago, but a local factory went out of business, and now people are unemployed and quite poor. Or, as was the case in the community served by the Banbury North School, a new economic base, coupled with the creation of new housing communities, rapidly made an area that was anything but wealthy into a place with different expectations, norms, and probable views about public schools. The perplexing reality is that different and often changing communities might be found immediately adjacent to one another. Schools within the same school district might often serve very different communities.

If a person is to be successful at pursuing a leadership position in any particular school or community, it is essential that he or she have a very clear understanding of the nature of the community's expectations for its local schools. A potential educational administrator must not only know the planks of his or her personal educational platform, as described in chapter 1, but also the platform of the community in which he or she wishes to work.

This chapter includes a number of strategies and techniques that you may wish to use as you begin to research the school in which you wish to sell and market your leadership skills.

WHY GO LOOKING?

There is no such thing as a perfect place to work. Of course, there is always a temptation to idealize some settings from afar, particularly if you are not satisfied with the place in which you now work. After all, "The grass is always greener. . . ." But it is critical to remember the point of that proverb: Often, you discover that the ideal features of another place do not meet your expectations, and that it would have been better to stay at the place from which you started.

Despite this warning that you may not be completely satisfied in your choice of a new work environment, however, there may be reasons why you choose to look in new places when you want to set forth as a beginning administrator.

Many individuals decide to stay in the school or district in which they have had most, if not all, of their teaching experience; such a choice makes a good deal of sense from a number of perspectives. First, you would not have to move your residence. Anyone who has gone through the hassle of selling a house, buying (or renting) another home, and dealing with the frustration and aggravation of packing, moving, and unpacking rarely looks forward to a repeat performance. A second advantage of staying where you have always worked is that you know the turf. In general, you are likely to be much more aware of the traditions, customs, policies, and procedures if you take an administrative post at "home." Third, relocating from one district to another may result in serious negative consequences to your retirement benefits. This is an even bigger concern if you move to a different state.

What are some additional advantages that you see in remaining patient and seeking an administrative position in the school or district where you have spent a great deal of time as a teacher?

_____

_____

_____

_____

By contrast, there are also compelling reasons for people to look for a first administrative position far from where they have spent time as a classroom teacher. Perhaps the strongest of these is the belief that it is quite difficult to take on a position of authority and control over people who have been your professional peers and colleagues in the recent past. Many administrators report that they would never want to be a principal in the same school in which they had worked as a teacher, because they realize that stepping from one professional role to another often causes one to lose valued friendships. Simply stated, it is exceptionally difficult to move into a position in which one may find it necessary to professionally evaluate personal friends, particularly if negative findings from the evaluation process are likely.

Are there other reasons why you would not like to step into an administrative role in a school in which you have recently served as a classroom teacher?

_____

_____

_____

_____

For the most part, decisions about the right places to seek an administrative appointment are matters of personal preference. There is no research base to guide you in this matter. Keep in mind, however, that educators who began their careers in rural settings tend to stay in similar places throughout their careers. The same is true for people with a lot of experience in either urban or suburban settings. You may get an idealized sense that, if you have spent the first ten or more years of your career as a teacher in the inner city, it might be a good thing to seek out a life in the peace and quiet of the country. But you may feel uncomfortable there and may regret that decision, much as might a rural educator who goes off to find adventure in the city.

When you begin to think about the broad issues described here, namely the questions of why you want to move into administration, and why you want to relocate (or not) in order to pursue a career goal, you may wish to return to your personal educational platform and reflect again on the most critical values that drive your behavior. There are likely many times when you can pursue jobs that may pay more, offer better fringe benefits, put you in a more prestigious setting, or give you greater professional visibility, but the best choice must be based on what you value. For example, will moving to a new community disrupt your family to the extent that you and all around you will be miserable?

In considering such choices, you may wish to take a few moments to look at your platform and to note in the space below some of the most central personal issues that you do not wish to compromise as you look for new professional opportunities.

_____

_____

_____

_____

SIZING UP THE POSSIBLE SETTING

When you make the initial decision to set sail toward challenges in a new setting, you have to consider a number of issues that are likely to affect your marketing strategy. There are two basic ways to consider the issue of setting. One is in terms of whether the setting is truly consistent with your personal interests and taste. The second is in terms of whether the target setting is a place where your particular skills and talents can be used effectively.

Do You Want to Work There?

Earlier in this chapter, it was suggested that the old adage "The grass is always greener . . ." may or may not be true when it comes to looking for an administrative post. Your perception of a tranquil lifestyle in a bucolic setting may not be what you really want if you have spent most of your life in Manhattan or Chicago. The hustle, bustle, and energy of San Francisco or New Orleans may not really thrill you if you have spent your personal and professional life in Southwest Wisconsin or the Panhandle of Texas.

As you begin to look at possible locations for an administrative position, particularly if that position is located in a community in which you have had little experience or with which you have had little direct contact, consider the importance that quality of life will have for you. Do you want to fight traffic each day? Are there shopping centers available in the area? Are there good restaurants? What about a church that you would want to attend? If you have children, what do you know about the schools that they would attend in the community? One English headteacher, or principal, once stated that he would not take a post in a town "if it didn't have a church, a school, or a pub with really good food." You may not have much feeling about any of those three civic virtues, but what may be some of the features in your ideal community?

_____

_____

_____

_____

Before you send in an application for a job at a school, what are the features of the school in which you would like to serve as a principal? Consider some broad issues at first. For example, if you have little (or no) experience working in a middle school, would you consider such a placement if it were offered? Even if your whole career has been spent in high schools, remember that some school districts may want a person with that background to take over a middle school or junior high school. Although your administrative credential may permit that and although you may receive a solid employment offer to "step down" to a school that many consider to be beneath a high school in stature, would you really consider that kind of opportunity?

Numerous other issues should be considered about any school with an advertised opening for a principalship. For example, with what grade levels of students are you interested in working? What about the enrollment of your ideal school? If you could choose the types of teacher characteristics found in a school where you would serve, what would they be?

What are some of the many issues that you would want to know about a particular school before you might entertain an offer for employment there?

_____

_____

_____

_____

Now that you have reviewed the pluses of the school or district in which you would agree to serve as a principal, what about the downside of things? What features of a school or community would be so contrary to your views and values that you would not wish to work there? As you consider these issues, please remember that you are not likely to be extremely effective in your principalship if you are not happy with your placement. On the surface, a particular position may look great because of the salary, reputation of the school, fringe benefits, or many similar variables. But, just like a piece of beautiful designer clothing that does not fit right, the wrong school or district will not be comfortable and will not make you happy.

What are some reasons why you would not be interested in a particular school or community?

_____

_____

_____

_____

_____

THE COMMUNITY'S NEEDS

A school district is going to hire a person to be an administrator because there is a belief that the administrator has something to give to the school or district. In short, you may have great interests in a particular job, but no one is going to hire you because of your interests alone. What can you do for the organization?

For any particular school in which you have an interest in seeking an administrative position, what are some of your special strengths and skills that you believe can contribute to that school and help it achieve its goals?

_____

_____

_____

_____

_____

There is no one who will ever be a totally perfect match for a given job. In fact, there are some reasons that would make you (or any other applicant) not a particularly effective choice for an administrative post. Although it is very important for you to know what your strengths are, it is equally critical to understand your limitations. For example, if you are not comfortable with financial management or budgeting, would you really like to be placed in a position in which skill in these areas is absolutely essential for success?

What do you believe are some of your limitations as a potential candidate for an administrative post?

_____

_____

_____

_____

_____

As a result of your understanding some of your limitations, what might be some settings in which you believe you would experience a great deal of difficulty or frustration if asked to serve as a school administrator?

_____

_____

_____

_____

The purpose of asking these last two questions is not to shake your confidence or to suggest that going into an administrative position may not be right for you. It is assumed that you have already considered the pros and cons of taking this career path. Assessing your limitations in terms of taking on certain administrative tasks is done for two reasons. First, if you can now identify some areas in which you need to learn more (e.g., budgeting or financial management), that will give you some clear direction for further professional growth and development. Second, you do not want to walk into a situation in which you are not likely to succeed, particularly if this is your first administrative assignment. In short, the best career moves and decisions are often those that are *not* made at first.

LEARN ABOUT THE CUSTOMER: A FEW TIPS

In the scenario that opened this chapter, Alicia Dillsworth really walked into a tough situation. It was certainly not because she had not taken steps to get a feel for what the issues were likely to be in her new school and district; her only problem was that her analysis did not pick up some relatively recent changes in the nature of the school and district. Reviewing some of the things that Alicia did can be an effective way for you to develop some skills at learning what your potential customers, (employing school districts) may want or need.

Here are a few tips to help you in looking at the place where you may end up working. Some of these things were done by Alicia in the scenario, and some were not.

1. Do your homework: read. When you find an opening in a community with which you are not familiar, read about the place in very general terms. Get out a road map for the area. Look at what is near the community. Is it likely to be a rural area, as suggested by its placement on the map? Or is it a suburb of a larger community? Even more interesting might be looking at whether a community might soon become a suburb. As urban sprawl affects more and more large cities in this country, more rural areas will be pulled into metropolitan communities.

2. Do your homework: read some more. After you have done some basic reconnaissance on a possible site by learning its location, size, population, major industries, and a number of other issues that can be downloaded from the Internet or found in an almanac, learn about the more subtle aspects of life in the community. One of the strategies that Alicia followed in this regard was to check out recent stories in the community's newspaper over a few weeks. What are some of the big issues likely to face you as a new principal or assistant principal? Is there news about how a new industrial park has just opened with a lot of high-paying technical jobs? When you are reading the recent issues of the newspaper, check out the editorial page. Columns and letters to the editor there can give you some important insights into local controversies, many of which are likely to have an impact on your work if you accept a position in the community. In addition to reading the newspaper, call the local chamber of commerce (if the community has one) and ask to receive any descriptive brochures they

may have. In short, look at the way your potential new home markets itself while you, in turn, develop a strategy to market your talent to them.

3. Talk to people who know the community. If the school and district is relatively close to where you now reside, there is a good chance that you will already know someone who has been there as a teacher, counselor, parent, or administrator, or in some other capacity. Ask their opinions about the place where you have an interest. Talk to your principal or assistant principal, particularly if the school to which you may apply is in the same athletic conference. Principals talk to one another, and there are networks that can be helpful to you in an indirect way. Call a real estate agent and ask about the cost of housing. Also, what can the agent (as a representative of the local business community) tell you of substance about what is going on in the schools? Do not simply call and ask if the schools are good, as real estate agents tend to be generous in their descriptions of the quality of life in communities in which they want to sell houses. Ask for more detail than simply an opinion about the general quality of the schools.

4. Check the school profile on the Internet. Most states now require local school districts to publish important student achievement data in the form of Community Report Cards at least once per year. State departments of education gather this information and generally make it quite easy for outsiders to access information about attendance, standardized test scores, dropout rates, annual average per-pupil expenditures for schools, and so forth. Keep in mind that even if the data you find are not particularly positive, the school may still be a great place to work. Remember that it is often a good idea to start a career in a place where things can only get better.

5. See for yourself. There is no substitute for going on-site yourself and looking around. Before any interview takes place, or perhaps before you send a formal application to a district, take a trip there and look things over for yourself. There may be some buildings that are in need of so much repair, for example, that you may have no time to do anything in terms of educational improvement. Or, your potential school may be a living nightmare in terms of possible student health and standards issues; you may have to deal with local drug pushers who have taken over apartments across the street from your school. What about a school located on a

major highway, with few apparent safety precautions being taken to keep students out of the path of oncoming cars? There are simply some challenges that you may not wish to take on, particularly as a rookie. In addition to looking at your possible school, "hang out" a bit in the community to get a better feel for what it would be like to work there. Have lunch in a local restaurant, or go to the closest mall. Get a true feel for the community.

What are some other strategies that you believe you would follow in getting an accurate picture of what a community, school district, or individual school might be like?

_____

_____

_____

_____

_____

CHAPTER SUMMARY

This chapter addressed the important issue of determining the characteristics of a school or district before you actually apply for an administrative position. This is a more critical issue should you decide to proceed with an application or have a strong desire to land a job in that district or school. Nothing is more damaging to a person during an interview for a job than to suddenly be trapped by questions that reveal a lack of knowledge about the place where the person wishes to work. On the other hand, choosing a target carefully will alert you to whether or not you wish to take on the challenge of trying to provide effective leadership in a particular school.

CHAPTER 3

Choosing the Target

After two and one-half years of racing over to Mt. Simon University to take afternoon classes after work, Spencer Rockaway had finally received his master's degree in educational administration, along with his state elementary school principal's certificate. Although he had only five years of teaching experience, he felt ready, willing, and able to go out into the job market and become a building administrator. Being a principal would be nice, but Spencer was realistic enough to know that, at his age and with his experience, he would more likely be seen as a candidate for an assistant's job.

When Spencer started to review the job openings posted in the *Mt. Simon Placement Newsletter*, the state principals' association weekly job lists, and the classified ads in *Education Week*, he felt like the proverbial kid in a candy shop. The local lists included openings for assistants and principals in just about every part of the state, and there were openings posted in the national publications for jobs all over the country. As Spencer was really a "local kid" who had grown up not very far from where he went to college and where he now taught, he began to imagine the possibilities that lay in a complete change of scenery. Besides, he did not have a family, so considerations about where his kids would go to school or where his spouse might find a job did not concern him at the moment. It would be a good time to make a choice, move out, and start a whole new life wherever he could find a suitable job and an area where he would like to live.

Spencer had grown up on a small farm here in the Midwest. Thoughts of leaving the plains and going to southern California or New England occupied his thinking almost all day long for several weeks. His fifth grade students even began to see that he was now distracted by something outside the classroom. They really loved Mr. Rockaway, and they could see that something was on his mind.

Spencer started clipping out the newspaper announcements for jobs that really caught his fancy. He began sending out copies of his résumé all over the country, along with letters of application. He was so intrigued by the descriptions of some districts in the ads that he called several districts to request copies of their application forms. In total, he made contact with about thirty school systems in eleven states. The district that was farthest from his present home was near San Diego, and the one closest to him was in his own state: a prestigious district just outside his home state's largest city. Although his own school district had two openings for assistant principals for the coming year, Spencer did not apply for those.

Suddenly, the phone began to ring, and Spencer began to get form letters from several of the districts, saying that he was being considered among the finalists for their openings. Most of the positions were for assistant principals in elementary or middle schools. He did get a few "bites" from districts that saw him as a potential candidate for a principalship, but he started realizing that most of those were very small, rural districts in the Midwest, and he wanted to work in very different surroundings next year. Of course, he also received a number of polite form letters from schools that noted that he was "one of many outstanding applicants, but at this time. . . ."

Spencer now took out the map of the United States on which he had circled the locations of all the districts to which he had applied. As he started to realize that he might be a serious candidate in many locations, he had a sudden panic attack. "What if they really want me to be an assistant principal in the San Diego area, or in Vermont? I've only seen those places on television, and I don't even know if I can afford to fly there for the job interview if I'm invited!" Then he also had another thought. "If I get a chance to go to that ritzy suburb up north here in my home state, I'll probably hate it. I never go near that place because of the traffic, crime rate, and everything else." The kid in the candy shop was suddenly aware that he didn't like some types of bubble gum and licorice, and certain types of nuts on his candy bars.

Spencer Rockaway is having the same thoughts that many individuals have when they first set out on the trail to get experience as school administrators. He is young, full of ambition, interested in seeing the world, and filled with romantic notions of how things might be in other places. He is also able to think about simply picking up and moving anywhere because he does not have family responsibilities at this point in his life. And the fact is, as school districts begin to more fully realize the problem of increasing shortages of administrative personnel, they may start advertising nationally and presenting the more marketable features of their school systems as enticements to teacher and administrator applicants. It is indeed a buyer's market these days, but it is also a time to recall the old saying "Buyer beware."

This chapter will lead you through a consideration of several issues before sending an application for an administrative position in a particular school or district. As was true of Spencer Rockaway in the opening scenario, a temptation for many who are seeking their first post is to apply for every opening that comes out in the placement listings of the local university, or the classified ads in *Education Week*, or the announcements posted with the state administrators' or school boards' associations. In an effort to get a first assistant principalship or principalship, people often "shotgun" applications all over the place. They might be like Spencer Rockaway, who saw the job search as an opportunity to look for a perfect job in some faraway part of the United States, thus satisfying a desire to be an administrator in some idealized setting. More commonly, though, people tend to confine their job searches to schools and districts within a reasonable distance from their present residence. In any case, the obvious problem with either type of strategy is that an applicant may be offered a position in a place where he or she has no real interest in working. Later in this chapter, we will consider this problem more completely.

Rather than using a shotgun technique, this chapter strongly recommends that you make use of fine, "surgical" techniques in looking for the job you want. As is true in marketing products in the corporate world, companies do not waste their time, their money, and the goodwill of possible customers by "throwing" their products at everyone. Snowblowers are not likely to sell well in Tucson or El Paso, so stores in those communities rarely stock or display these items, although they would sell well in Denver or Milwaukee. Ads for amusement parks are not as frequent in communities with a high percentage of senior citizens. Individuals marketing their talents must learn these lessons of selective selling as a way to economize and save resources (time, money, and energy) and also to maximize the potential of achieving a successful sale.

WHERE TO BEGIN

As noted in chapter 1, the logical place for any marketing campaign to begin is with an appreciation of the nature of the product to be sold. This is true in the marketing of snowblowers or of swimming pools (not an easy sell in Buffalo or Boston) and, even more important to your immediate concerns, in the potential sale of your talent as a school leader. One of the most important parts of appreciating your personal values and beliefs is that it can help you understand what is and is not important in the choice of where you might work.

Consider again the case of Spencer Rockaway. He was a young man from a rural background in a farming community. Although that statement in itself is not enough to tell all of his deepest values and beliefs, it is still enough to provide some insights into the type of setting in which he might discover that working would be uncomfortable. To suddenly realize that he would not like the traffic and potential crime found in a large city should not be a surprise. To be sure, there are many people who grew up in small towns and who have succeeded in places like New York and Chicago, but the potential for unhappiness in such transplants is often great. As a Midwesterner who has apparently not traveled around the country, Spencer seemed enamored with a personal vision of what life would be like in an area like San Diego or New England, but he may not have turned out to be happy there.

Most people looking for a first job are not like Spencer, with his determination to try to find a job "anywhere but here." The majority of individuals looking for an initial placement as an administrator are likely to want to stay in their own districts, or at least to stay close enough to home to feel comfortable. That is not always simply because they have families for whom a move would be difficult; it is sometimes simply their preference. Even so, it is important to know one's personal preferences in terms of lifestyle and surroundings before moving to the next county, or even the other side of the same school district.

List a handful of features of your current lifestyle and community that you value strongly enough to try to make certain that these characteristics are present in the next place where you live. For example, is living in a community near mountains important? How about being close to an ocean shore? Do you like living in the desert enough that you would want to make sure you can do that in the future? What about living close to family?

_____

_____

_____

_____

_____

Now, consider what characteristics about a community you would find so undesirable that you would probably never want to live there. For example, are winters too cold, summers too hot, or rain insufficient in an area you are considering? Do you want to make certain that you will not be faced with a long commute each day? Is the total absence of any hills or mountains a major drawback?

_____

_____

_____

_____

_____

Most of the items included in the lists you just made probably deal with broad characteristics of desirable or undesirable communities and are in very general terms. You now have thought out some reasons you would hate to leave the Midwest, the Southwest, the Northeast, or the deep South. But there are other issues to consider as you select the appropriate target area for your job searching.

PROFESSIONAL VALUES AND OTHER ISSUES

As stated previously, the majority of administrative job seekers are unlikely to be thinking in terms of long-distance moves, say from Illinois to California or Massachusetts. For most educators, the job search process will be limited to considering positions in their current states. This makes sense, as certification and licensure is a state-by-state issue. Further, many job seekers are concerned about the ability to carry over their retirement plans, and that is also a function of the state in which one begins one's teaching career. Theoretically, it may be nice to think of an educational system without state boundaries so that potential administrators could more easily be recruited nationally and not just locally. But for at least the time being, there are many reasons why people look more locally for new jobs.

Even within the same state where you have worked for many years, there can be enormous differences between one community and school district and another. As has been noted, some communities are rural, some are urban, and there are many suburban districts. Pay range seems most often to follow district size, or at least proximity to larger urban areas; simply stated, you get paid more to be a principal of an urban or suburban school than you might in most rural schools. And all three choices might be located only a few miles apart in the same state.

Having made these observations about choice based on district characteristics (and salary differential), once again, it is also extremely important to review your personal value statement and educational platform to determine whether a good match exists between you and the values espoused in a particular community.

In terms of a match between your personal values and a place to work, what are three or four aspects of life in a particular community that would be most consistent with some of the beliefs and values that you have? For example, is a small town with strong church communities extremely important? What about the presence of private schools?

_____

_____

_____

_____

What are some things you might find in a community that would be completely against some of your personal beliefs and values? For example, would a city's reputation for a high crime rate be enough to deter you from pursuing a position in a particular location?

_____

_____

_____

_____

There are also practices in a particular school that might be contrary to your personal sense of values. Consider, for example, a school district in which corporal punishment is widely used inviting you to join their administrative team as an assistant principal in a middle school. Would you be willing to use the paddle on a student? What are some practices that might be used in a school or district that would be so contrary to your beliefs that you would not wish to work in that setting?

The temptation to jump at the first job that is offered to you is a great one. You have spent time and money getting ready for a career in administration, so it may be easy to ignore some things that will eventually cause you a great deal of frustration. Does the school system make use of any curricular or instructional practices with which you are not comfortable? Approaches to discipline that you believe to be ineffective? Remember, this is the time to form a clear idea in your mind of what is or is not acceptable. You are likely to be in the school that you select for a few years. If you decide that what you wanted to see during the application process is not at all the reality that exists after you sign a contract, you are going to be in the difficult situation faced by many who jump at the first offer that comes along: if you stay, you will be increasingly unhappy, but if you leave immediately, others may wonder what was wrong with your judgment in the first place. Worse yet, it may cause people to suspect that you were not effective in the job and that you had to leave prematurely for some reason. There is an old saying that "the best decisions made are often those not made at all." Think through all of the pros and cons of taking a particular professional role before you step into that position.

No school or district is likely to offer you an absolutely perfect job. There are probably going to be aspects of any position that are not exactly what you wanted to find during your job search. But you must still try to do everything in your power to review each possible career opportunity so that you do not feel that you have compromised certain personal values and beliefs by taking a job. Choose your target very carefully.

METHODS OF NARROWING THE TARGET

Ultimately, the decision whether you wish to work in a particular school or district is yours alone to make. It is important to note how comfortable you feel in an environment in which you may potentially spend several years as a school administrator. Following are some strategies that might make your selection of the proper target more effective.

1. Talk to people. As you start to identify "finalists" among the schools to which you have applied, you need to find individuals in each school to talk with about some of the daily practices that will possibly guide your life there. If you already know a few people in a school or district because you once worked with them, or because they took courses with you at a university, or in any other context, visit with them and find out what real life is like in their school. What are some of the traditions, norms, and other aspects of the prevailing culture of the school? Can you adjust to these features?

   If you are currently considering a position at a particular school or district, do you know anyone who might be a reliable source of information concerning the daily life in that organization?

   _____

   _____

   _____

   _____

   _____

   What kinds of things would you hope to learn from the people you already know in the school or district? How will this help you in making a decision whether or not to continue to pursue a job in that setting?

   _____

   _____

   _____

   _____

   _____

2. Listen carefully to subtle signals. During the interview stage, or simply in your initial conversations with district and school representatives, be very attentive to the things that are stated as well as the things that are not. Is there a pattern that develops? Do people subtly change the subject when you ask about such things as the working relationships with other administrators in the school or district? Do you notice that no one talks about the parents? Or the teachers' association?

   What have you learned about the schools in which you have an interest, based largely on the comments made (or not made) during interviews or other conversations related to the job for which you are applying?

_____

_____

_____

_____

_____

3. Become a skilled observer. Applying for a job asks you to become a type of qualitative or field researcher. Often, what you hear or read about in a school is not nearly as powerful a descriptor of reality as simply keeping your eyes wide open when you visit the scene. For example, in some schools, the students do not appear to be very happy. In other places, there are so many special drill sessions to help students pass the state achievement test that there appears to be little other focus in the school. What are the kinds of places where you are likely to be happy or fulfilled as a school administrator?

What are some of the nonverbal signals you might see in a school that would make it unlikely for you to be happy working in that environment in the future?

_____

_____

_____

_____

_____

CHAPTER SUMMARY

This chapter considered another critical aspect of an effective administrative job search. Rather than simply applying for and pursuing any job for which you might be even remotely qualified, it is strongly suggested that you have a duty to yourself—and probably any employing school district—to take a look at whether or not there is a good match between you and the school in which there is an opening. It is not simply a matter of whether or not you are going to be happy in a particular setting; rather, if you are to be a successful school leader, it is critical that you start a job with the notion that the place where you work is where you want to be. Under some circumstances, that may not always be possible, but whenever you can, take a look at the nature of the place to which you are applying and decide whether it is a place you want to be _at_, not _from_.

CHAPTER 4

Lining Up Your Ducks

When David Ramirez had completed his coursework at State University five years ago and qualified for his principal's certificate, he had wanted to find an assistant principalship in a school not too far from home. He had reasoned that it would be good to get about four or five years of experience as a practicing school administrator in order to be ready for the job of principal in the future. At that time, he had had a hard time finding a position that matched his interests. He had not wanted to have to commute too far each day, he had wanted to work in an elementary school, and he had mostly been interested in a suburban or rural setting. These demands had not seemed to be particularly difficult, but he had still had very few opportunities that seemed right.

As a result, David had taken the first job that came along, and he had regretted that decision ever since. He now worked as the assistant principal at Green Meadows Elementary School, the largest of three K–8 buildings in the Quail Hollow Community Schools. Green Meadows was only about twelve miles from Mason Grove, the town where David had worked for ten years as a fifth grade teacher. On paper, the school fit all of his requirements perfectly. Green Meadows was the right size (700 students), not far away, and represented a blend of rural and suburban characteristics. On the other hand, David was quite disappointed with the leadership of Howard Goalsby, the principal of the school since its opening seventeen years ago. Howard did little to help David learn some of the things that a principal should know. David learned quickly that when he came to his boss with questions about policies or procedures, he usually got one of two responses. One was that it was unwise to worry too much about policies because, as Howard would often say with a laugh, "I never paid much attention to that kind of stuff, and what did it hurt me?" The other was for Howard to simply look at David and tell him to "tough it out like I did when I was your age." David knew that Howard was not held in high esteem by his teachers, the other administrators in the district, or most parents. Still, Howard was "connected" to four of the school board members, with whom he played golf and drank beer regularly. He had been in the community for so long and knew the politics of the area so well that no one seemed to do anything contrary to his wishes. David felt as if he was now simply putting in his time and not really learning anything about leading a school.

As a result, David now began to look at making his next career move. He had always anticipated that, by this time in his life, he would be making a move toward his first principalship. But because he had not been able to gain much positive experience in Quail Hollow, he did not yet feel ready to step into the "hot seat." He started to think about a lateral move to another assistant principalship. When he contacted the state principals' association about possible openings for assistant principals, though, David was surprised to start getting some calls from districts that were interested not in his service as an assistant but that instead wondered whether he was interested in applying for a principal's position.

David was truly amazed at this turn of events. Just a few years ago, he had tried everything he could to find a few openings for assistant principalships. There were not many choices, and he also learned that the chances for stepping into a principalship at that time were practically nonexistent. Now, all he had to do was make a few inquiries about a building-level administrative position, and it seemed as if everyone was chasing him. Suddenly, David began to feel like a kid in a candy shop. His dream of becoming a principal was a lot closer to being realized than it was just a few months ago. People were asking him to think about a principalship! The question now no longer seemed to be whether he could be a principal someday; now, the only question appeared to be where.

Several important issues are raised in this brief scenario. First, David Ramirez is like you and many other individuals who may be at the beginning of their careers as school administrators. He has already made the leap from the classroom to the administrator's office. As may also be true in your case, he has paid his dues in making that transition. He spent some time in the classroom before he made the choice to leave a world that he loved and seek new challenges in professional education.

Like you, he invested a great deal of time, money, and energy in pursuing graduate courses at a local university where he studied the subjects needed to qualify him for a master's degree and for certification in his state as a school administrator. He prepared for and successfully completed a written examination required by the state department of education. Finally, he applied for and received the credentials needed to serve as a principal or assistant principal. Above all, he made a psychological commitment to leave the classroom—a world he knew, enjoyed, and felt comfortable in—to step into the administrative suite, a new world filled with unknown variables.

Another lesson found in the story of David Ramirez is that, like many who are first entering the world of school administration, he wanted to do it as quickly as possible, but he also wanted to do it on his own terms to some extent. He wanted to stay close to home, in a specific role, in a particular size and type of school, and presumably with a reasonable salary. When he took his first assistant principalship, he knew he wanted to seek a new job, but he wanted to be in control of the process. In David's case, what he believed to be an ideal position turned sour when he discovered that he really did not have all that he needed in order to be successful.

As he developed a rational plan for seeking a more suitable placement, David discovered yet another fact of administrative career development. Although he considered himself to be ready to seek only another assistant principalship, the education community had a different view. In recent years, the number of qualified applicants for principalships has dwindled so much that it is, in fact, a seller's market. If a person is not particularly demanding in terms of a specific location, district type and size, minimum pay, and so forth, it is quite likely that an offer for a principalship will be remarkably quick in coming. David therefore discovered another reality, namely that some opportunities may arise without any type of foreshadowing or warning. What started out as a search for a more interesting assistant principalship quickly became an opportunity to become a principal. At this point in the story, "all the best laid plans" are seemingly about to "go awry."

David Ramirez has a huge choice to make now. He has to make a choice that he did not anticipate needing to consider at this juncture of his career. He also has to face the even more critical issue of whether he will now step out of a strategic, planned, proactive approach to managing his career and suddenly assume a much more reactive stance. In short, will he now jump at an opportunity he did not anticipate? In this current era of principal shortages across the nation, this is an issue that you may need to consider much more frequently and carefully than you had expected.

All of these issues point to the central theme in this chapter, namely, how does a person seeking a job in the field of school administration take steps to ensure that he or she controls the process?

DUCK HUNTING

Hunters realize that the most fundamental issue associated with their sport is finding the prey they want to hunt in the first place. Simply taking a crossbow or a shotgun out into the woods to see if you can hunt down some type of animal may be necessary if you are simply looking for something to eat that day, but most sporting hunters have a more precise set of goals in mind. They are deliberately hunting ducks, or deer, or another specific kind of animal. That focus will help the hunter to be well prepared by selecting the right type of weapon, location, ammunition, season of the year, and, perhaps most importantly, the right kind of hunting license. Looking for an administrative job may not require you to don camouflage clothing or sit in a duck blind at dawn while making quacking sounds. But you still need to consider many of the other issues hunters need to deal with.

The Right License

Game wardens frown on people who try to hunt elk but only have a fishing license or on people who have a license that is the proper type but is expired. You may not be fined or imprisoned if you go out to find an administrative position with the wrong kind of license, but you could be wasting a lot of time and money by not preparing in this area.

If you are looking for a principalship (and normally an assistant principalship as well), it is fair to assume that the hunting license you will need is a state principal's certificate or license. Note these tips to avoid getting nabbed by the warden (or a personnel director in a school district) for an embarrassing or disqualifying error:

1. Make sure that your administrative credentials are up to date. Often, people wait a few years after completing an administrative certification or licensing program before they get out into the job

market and start hunting for a job. In all probability, the credential for which you may have qualified a year or two ago is still valid, but check it first. During the past few years, most states have made changes related to teacher and administrator certification. In some states, this might only mean that your certificate is now called a license. But in other cases, time limits may have been imposed on how long an initial certificate or license may be kept prior to its first use. In other words, you may find that a state has adopted a "use it or lose it" clause to give schools new teachers and administrators who come from more recently completed preparation programs. The rationale for this is found in cases in which people may have completed a course in school law or some other subject ten or more years ago: arguably, basic principles of law (or finance, or personnel management) do not change overnight, but legal precedents based on court decisions can and do change frequently.

Another case in which you may get caught unexpectedly in a "time warp" may come from settings where specific credentials that formerly covered certain jobs may have changed since you last checked. For example, you may have completed a principal certification program that was sufficient for certification at all levels of schooling, pre-K–12. During the past few years, though, your state may have changed policies to require applicants for a secondary school certificate to have had experience as a teacher in a secondary school. The same might be true of elementary or middle school certification.

Perhaps the most critical thing to remember about verifying your certification and license is that this task should be done well before you apply for any position. Like the duck hunter, you cannot get the right license after you have set out into the field.

If you currently have an administrative certificate or license, note the details of that credential in terms of expiration date, levels of schooling covered, and so forth.

_____

_____

_____

_____

2. Check the laws of the state where you want to work. If you are planning to find a job some distance away from where you

have worked as a teacher or from where you completed your initial certification, check the licensing requirements in your new area. Some state departments have certification reciprocity agreements with neighboring states, but many others do not. It is your responsibility to check out this type of issue before you apply for a job. Simply assuming that, because Ohio borders Indiana and Kentucky, you can easily get a certificate in any of those states because you completed an administrator preparation program at Ohio State University might be a very faulty assumption. You need to call the office of teacher and administrator certification in the state department of education in any state where you hope to work and make certain that you qualify for a certificate. If not, you will need to find out precisely how to qualify for the appropriate license as soon as possible. Personnel directors in hiring school systems expect that you will be ready to step into a position as soon as it is offered, without problems concerning certification.

What states (if any) have reciprocity with your current state? If you are looking into jobs in other states, what are their specific requirements for certification or licensure as a school administrator?

_____

_____

_____

_____

The Right Ammunition

Trying to catch fish with a shotgun is not a terribly wise approach to the sport. In fact, it is a terrible example of overkill. The same is true of trying to land an administrative job with the wrong strategies. Imagine an individual applying for an entry-level administrative position with an application form, a letter of interest in the advertised job, and two volumes of supporting information in three-ring binders. Also, think of your reaction as a reviewer of dozens of applications if that same applicant were to include letters of recommendation from eight or nine people when the application materials ask only for the names and phone numbers of three individuals who might be contacted concerning the applicant.

If you were a member of a committee reviewing applications for an administrative position in your school or district, how would you react to the kind of overkill demonstrated by the overzealous applicant described here?

_____

_____

_____

_____

Among the terms that you might have used in your answer are "angry," "annoyed," or even "disappointed because the applicant did not read the directions." All are quite understandable when people feel pressured by an applicant. In fact, this type of overkill may even trigger concerns in reviewers about whether the applicant is trying to hide deficiencies by "snowing" the school system. Those making employment decisions want to make certain that they hire people with the sense needed to read instructions, decide what is needed, and then follow through. Tons of paper, recommendations, lists of awards, and similar materials can detract from an otherwise bona fide application by a qualified candidate. Use the right ammunition for the job.

The Right Location

The old saying about the grass always seeming greener on the other side of the fence really begins to make sense when thinking about looking for new jobs in new settings. As noted in chapter 3, identifying the right place to find a new job is extremely important. Using the hunting metaphor developed in this chapter, looking for a job in the wrong place is like trying to hunt for elk in the southwestern deserts of the United States: you simply will not be very successful. In the previous chapter, you were given some tips for selecting the right place for your job search based largely on your personal preferences: Do you prefer a rural community or a suburban setting? Do you want a warm year-round climate, or do you like to shovel snow?

In considering a "right" location in the context of this chapter, you will be focusing on selecting the correct professional setting for you. Do you want to work in a school that is similar to ones in which you have worked as a teacher, for example? What about the past performance of the school on selected academic indicators? For instance, do you want to work in a school that has always had a positive reputation in terms of students' achievement? If so, remember that there are often very high parental and community expectations accompanying that past performance. On the other hand, do you want to take on the challenge of leading a school where past test scores and other indicators have been low? Do you want to try to make a difference in a school that has traditionally not been viewed as successful?

What are some general characteristics of schools in which you would like to work as a principal or assistant principal, given your choice of several settings?

_____

_____

_____

_____

What about the community in which you will serve as a school administrator? There are many very pleasant places to work where there seems to be sufficient money and local pride in the public schools. Then again, there are settings where it will be very difficult to get everything that you immediately need. Both types of communities (and thousands of others in between those two opposites) have certain attractions as well as numerous negative features. "Rich" districts often carry the price tag of community members with unrealistic expectations for the schools and highly intrusive behavior by parents and other citizens. "Poor" communities can often have extremely supportive parents and other community members who will do whatever they can to help their children succeed.

If you could pick a perfect general community setting in which to work as a school administrator, describe it in the space that follows.

_____

_____

_____

_____

When considering the right community for you, remember to reflect again on the issues that were raised in chapter 3. Consider your personal and professional values and priorities and decide whether or not they may be compromised in the wrong setting.

PREPARING THE SCENE BACKSTAGE

Although it may not quite fit the hunting metaphor presented throughout this chapter, there is yet another area in which it is critical to prepare before you begin a serious search for a new professional position: the backstage area. Remember that any school or district that may be interested in hiring you will be inquiring about your abilities. They will be checking references and also current and past employers. As a result, there are certain things that you need to do in order to ensure that your application will be positively reviewed.

Select the Right References

There are many who will note that potential employers may not take very seriously the input of references provided by a job applicant. After all, references are likely to be carefully selected because they will say nothing but very positive things about a candidate. Regardless of the validity of this conventional wisdom, it is absolutely critical that you give appropriate consideration to who will be on your reference list. Potential employers will probably contact some or all of the people you provide.

The first critical thing is to make certain that you do, in fact, select people who will provide a positive review of your work. Often, applicants include people with whom they have had little or no contact for quite some time. For example, you may be inclined to select a principal with whom you worked when you first became a teacher. That principal may have been the person who inspired you to think about a career in school administration. In fact, it may have been he or she who commented to you about your potential as a great future principal someday. But remember that, after ten years or more, that person may no longer remember you as the bright young rising star. You may still cling to the notion that your first principal was totally sold on your ability, but memories fade. In short, whomever you select as a potential reference should be reviewed according to the following criteria:

1. Can the person speak to precise examples of your ability to carry out an assigned job? Often, we hear someone talk about our potential for someday, and we believe that such a statement is meant as a lifetime endorsement of capability to do a job effectively.

There is a huge difference between statements regarding potential and descriptions of actual accomplishment. A school district willing to hire you as a member of its administrative team wants someone to actually perform the job. They are not looking for someone who might become competent in a few years. You need to select references who can provide specific, concrete examples of how you are able to perform.

Who are some of the references that you might include who can provide concrete examples of your ability to perform job-related skills and duties?

_____

_____

_____

_____

2. Who are some individuals who can provide positive references as to your character and integrity? Although it is important to have people who can give examples of your ability to do the job, it is equally important to include references who can speak about your values. After all, serving as a school leader requires a person to possess certain characteristics indicative of high morals and integrity. Are you honest? Loyal? Faithful? Obviously, you will not just get a job simply because you fit a profile indicative of such lofty character traits. But you will not get a chance if people cannot talk about the inner side of you as a person. Employers want to hire people who can do the job, but they also want people who are decent and trustworthy employees.

Who are some individuals who can serve as positive character references and be included in your list of references?

_____

_____

_____

_____

3. What will you do about those who would not say positive things about you? There is a very important reality about growing older. As you do, you probably make enemies as well as friends. Whether that's your fault or not is unimportant. The fact is that there are likely to be people who have negative things to say about you, and while you are engaged in a job search, they may become serious liabilities to your efforts to move on. An "enemy" can be a teacher who worked next door to you and who felt that

you did not teach your classes as he or she might have preferred. Or it could be a department chair who always thought you showed him or her up. It could be a professor who did not like the questions you asked in class. If you have been in an administrative role before, it is likely that you had to discipline someone, and that person may be waiting for the opportunity to let others know how much you are not liked. The fact is, if you have been doing your job effectively over the years, you probably have a list of people whom you personally would never ask to serve as references.

Who are some people who, if you had the choice, would not be contacted by the school or district to which you are applying? Why not?

_____

_____

_____

_____

If people checking references do contact those with a less than favorable attitude toward you, how will you deal with the negative comments that might be made? Remember to be factual and honest in these situations. Avoid the temptation to try to damage the references' credibility. Two sets of negative assessments do not help anything.

_____

_____

_____

_____

_____

Be Proactive

In choosing references, recruit people who can actively help your cause. If you are really interested in a particular job (and hopefully, any job for which you apply should be one that really interests you!), line up some people who would be willing to call key people in the employing district to put in a good word for you. For example, you may have a former coworker who now works in your target school district in an administrative capacity. You may wish to let that person know that you want to work with him or her as a colleague administrator and ask if he or she can give you any help. A local university professor may be working with the district in which you want to serve. Can that person help you?

Who are some individuals that you may contact to help you in your pursuit of a particular job, even if they are not formally listed as references? In what specific ways could they assist you?

_____

_____

_____

_____

A word of caution is needed here. As you contact key people who might be of some assistance to you in a particular setting, be careful that you do not press too hard. For example, your best friend might be the president of the local school board in your target district, but stay away from any situation that appears as if you are trying to make use of pressure tactics. Nothing can sour a superintendent's interest in a candidate faster than being worried about whether a newly hired principal or assistant principal has connections with the board, some local politicians in a community, the state education department, or other similar entities.

CHAPTER SUMMARY

This chapter included a number of tips to help you set an effective stage for finding the right administrative job. The model that was suggested involved the steps that might be taken by a hunter who is seeking a particular type of game. When you are seeking a position, care must be taken to set up the groundwork needed before you get into the field. Nothing is more aggravating for a school system, for example, than to discover late in the search process that an apparently strong candidate cannot qualify for a job because he or she does not possess the right administrative credential.

Other suggestions were also offered to assist you in pursuing a job. For example, do not take references for granted. And also be prepared for a school system to discover that someone in your past does not necessarily think that you walk on water.

None of the steps offered here will guarantee that you will always get just the job that you want, where you want it, or when you want it. But ignoring these techniques will likely serve to block your chances for many successful job applications.

CHAPTER 5

Presentation Skills:
Portfolios for Professional Development

Davis Gray had spent most of the past several weeks reviewing all the job openings and descriptions that had been put out for school principalship openings in this part of his state. He had been an assistant principal here in Harlan Junction for four years, and he now wanted to move up further in the world of administration. Both he and his principal believed that he was ready for a school of his own, but in a small district like Harlan Junction, it would probably be many years before a job would come open for Davis. And so he began to apply in a number of other local school systems.

Many of the districts around Harlan Junction indicated that they were seeking professional portfolios from applicants. Davis had some notion of what that term implied, but he wanted to make certain that he knew what was really expected. He began to sort through his notes from graduate classes, newsletters from his state administrators' association, and other sources that he believed could provide him with some insights into what should be included in a professional portfolio. He also called Carla Chan, who had been an assistant in the district for eleven years and who always seemed to have some straight answers to Davis's questions. Carla simply stated that a professional portfolio is "some new educationese. All they want is for you to send them a ton of paper they can look through to make them feel as if they have attracted really important applicants for their principalships." Davis was not too sure that Carla really captured the idea very well, but he decided that he would spend the next few days going through his papers at home and in his office to find old letters from parents, pictures from the local newspapers, and other material that he could put into a notebook to send to the districts that asked for a portfolio. To be on the safe side, he was going to buy some very thick three-ring binders so that he could include as much material as possible. That would surely impress anyone seeking a portfolio.

Davis Gray may be an exception, but most educators have heard a good deal recently about the potential value of portfolios—as a "more authentic" way to present information about students' progress, or as a way for teachers to document personal professional development.

However, building your own portfolio can also assist you and other aspiring and experienced school administrators in at least three different and distinct areas: career planning, performance appraisal, and personal professional growth.

Although the suggestions included in this chapter vary according to the exact purpose of a portfolio, they represent neither a prescribed table of contents nor an arbitrary description of what a "proper" portfolio should look like. Some of the best portfolios are little more than simple three-ring binders, with sections clearly marked. And contrary to what Davis understood in the opening scenario, "a ton of paper" is not necessarily the best way to think about how to construct a useful portfolio. After all, the purpose of such a document should be to help you get a job, decide if you are doing a good job, or provide guidance to future career choices and patterns.

USING PORTFOLIOS TO GUIDE CAREER PLANNING

Portfolios can help you land an initial position, make a lateral career move, or seek a related position in administration such as a central office position or a superintendency. When developed for initial placement, the portfolio is best understood basically as a marketing tool used to sell two things to a school or district: your overall competence as an educator and, if you are just stepping into administration, your potential as a school administrator. Because many people move directly from classroom teaching into their first principalship, the portfolio must contain evidence of skill and dedication in the field of professional education, consistent with your own experiences.

In most cases, aspiring principals will have had little formal experience in management. If that is your situation, remember that you probably still possess two critical qualities that are highly valued by employing school systems. First, you are committed to education and the welfare of students. Second, even the least-experienced individuals probably have at least some degree of leadership ability. For example, you may have chaired some school or district committees, directed a major student activity, coached athletic teams, or been responsible for organizing special parent or community activities. Highlight these as a way of demonstrating that you do have leadership ability and experience.

If you do not yet have formal administrative experience, what are some concrete ways to demonstrate that you have had an active commitment to education and the needs of students?

_____

_____

_____

_____

_____

What are some ways that you have been able to demonstrate your leadership ability in support of your school or district?

_____

_____

_____

_____

_____

If you have experience as a school administrator, you may be interested in using a portfolio to help you move to a lateral career position. If that is the case, do not overlook the fact that, as with all educators, the portfolio may be a way to highlight your sincere commitment to the field of education. However, in contrast with your less-experienced colleagues, this is where you must market your experience and accomplishments as an educational leader.

As an experienced school administrator, what are some of your accomplishments that clearly demonstrate your ongoing commitment to education, students, and community service?

_____

_____

_____

_____

_____

What are some of your greatest accomplishments as an experienced school administrator?

Regardless of whether you are a beginner looking for your first administrative job or a veteran looking to make a change, the structure and sections of a portfolio for career planning will likely include the following sections:

1. Current résumé. More information will be included in the next chapter about this important document. But for now, note that it should be only a brief document that includes an outline of work experience, educational background, and any other items that you believe will give reviewers a quick understanding of your qualifications and characteristics.

2. Personal platform. As noted in chapter 1, the most important part of any marketing campaign is the identification of the product being sold. As you are the product in a job search, use your platform as a way to tell people what kind of person they are looking at for a position. The platform is a statement of your educational philosophy and values, similar to what politicians state as the kinds of things they will stand for if elected to office.

3. Professional credentials. Here, you should include copies of appropriate licenses, certificates, or endorsements that qualify you to apply for the position.

4. Transcripts. Something that is particularly important if you do not have an established prior record of administrative service is to show your potential to do a good job. One way to do this is by furnishing copies of transcripts that include details of completed graduate and undergraduate work.

5. Artifacts. If you are an experienced administrator seeking to make a move to a new setting, the artifacts to be included are examples of successful activities and programs that you have led. Make certain to select ones that appear to be related to the stated goals and objectives of the school or district to which you are applying. For example, you might include a brochure that you developed to describe a new program for latchkey children, or newspaper articles that described how you established an effec-

tive community involvement program. You could also provide summaries of achievement test scores in your school for the past year. Many different things can be included as indicators of your recent success as a leader.

If you have limited administrative experience, this portfolio section might include examples of accomplishments or current activities that show potential for strong future leadership. Examples might be new student programs that you initiated in your classroom, awards or other recognition for effective teaching, or reports from committees on which you served as either the chair or as an active member.

Regardless of your experience, this section of the portfolio may be the closest thing to a scrapbook collection. But take care that what is included is relevant and is not overwhelming to a reviewer. After all, tons of paper can serve to put people off. What you present in this section must be indicative of your likely success and effectiveness when the school board hands you the keys to a multimillion-dollar physical plant and the responsibility of overseeing the well-being of hundreds of students and teachers. Selecting a new principal or assistant principal is not a trivial matter, so ensure that the portfolio artifacts you include are serious and focused.

What are some artifacts you could include that would demonstrate to an employing school or district that you are capable of providing the kind of educational leadership that they are seeking?

_____

_____

_____

_____

_____

6. References. Again, what is included here must be related to your level of experience. If you have no formal administrative experience, you will need to include letters and statements indicating people's perceptions of your potential, if not your actual accomplishments. On the other hand, if you have experience, you will need to include letters that speak to specific indicators of success in administration. Notes saying that you are a nice person or are very personable are wonderful souvenirs to keep, but not in a

professional portfolio whose goal is to convince a potential employer that you have the ability to do a complex, difficult, and extremely important job. Every applicant can find people who are willing to provide endorsements of personal qualities. However, the best endorsements come from people who can talk about you as someone with great qualities who will also do an effective job in schools.

Who are some of the individuals you plan to include as references in your portfolio? Next to each named person, indicate the reasons why you intend to include him or her on your list.

_____

_____

_____

_____

_____

7. Other material. These might be items specifically required by a school system as part of the application process. For example, a district may ask an experienced applicant to include a description of the administrator evaluation system used in his or her last school system or a profile generated from participation in an assessment center.

An important word of caution about using a portfolio as part of the job searching process: you can include too much. There is often a temptation for beginners to disguise lack of experience in a sea of descriptions of trivial events. If you have never been a school administrator before, that fact will be apparent to reviewers, and some may actually appreciate that fact. Remember that no one can read a reviewer's mind. In a similar vein, if you are an experienced administrator, you need to avoid trying to "snow" interviewers and reviewers with a lot of information that may or may not tell them if you can do what is needed in a new setting.

PERFORMANCE APPRAISAL

One attractive feature of portfolios is that they can be used to guide your long-term performance appraisal as a leader. Currently, there is discontent around the nation with the ways in which principals and other administrators are being evaluated in many school systems. Evaluation is often described as a biased, arbitrary process influenced heavily by favoritism. As a result, an increasing number of districts have adopted portfolios as a way to increase individual input in principal evaluation, thus turning appraisal into a more useful activity focused on professional growth and improvement rather than personal judgment.

There are two distinct forms of personnel evaluation: formative assessment and summative assessment. The former has a goal of providing feedback so that individuals can modify their activities or behavior. The latter is a cumulative effort to evaluate a person's performance over a specific period. Regardless of the focus, there is relatively little difference in the structure of the portfolios used for formative or summative evaluation. The following components are suggested in both cases:

1. Résumé. This is only a brief presentation of basic information to enable reviewers to get a thumbnail picture of you.
2. Platform statement. This enables reviewers to gain insights into your personal and professional values.
3. Goal statements. This is the heart of the performance appraisal portfolio. Here, you should be able to articulate your short- and long-term professional goals. For example, you may identify important personal professional goals (e.g., "to increase elementary student achievement in math, as reflected by performance in the statewide achievement test"). These system-wide goals may overlap your individual goals, or may be viewed as extensions of what you want to do on your own. Regardless, they are goals that must be addressed as part of the appraisal process. The critical issue is to make a clear delineation between personal and institutional goals.
4. Assessment and reflection. Here, you might provide statements indicating the extent to which the goals identified in the previous section have been or are being achieved. These statements need to be tied to tangible evidence, not simply personal perceptions ("I believe the students in my school showed remarkable progress last year"), as they serve as the basis for future goal setting and professional development. In general, statements here must provide evidence of the extent to which goals were actually met ("mathematics achievement of third graders at Anytown School increased by an average of X percent last year, as reflected in performance on the statewide achievement test").

One caution should be noted. The purpose of this section is to provide accurate data about goals attained. It is not a place to boast about achievements. Obviously, it is important to put your best foot forward in presenting your accomplishments. But the assessment and reflection section is not a marketing tool to con people into perceiving effective performance where it does not exist.

5. Artifacts and evidence. This section contains the evidence to support any claims you made in the previous section of the portfolio. This might include a table showing math achievement test scores, or testimonials from a parent group complimenting you for an exceptional program promoting greater parent involvement. It is unlikely that a portfolio will have a neat one-to-one correspondence between goals and supporting artifacts, but it is critical that the significance of every item included is made clear. Include statements to let reviewers know why a particular letter, data table, or newspaper article was placed in the portfolio.

6. Other material. All portfolios can have a catchall section for information that does not quite fit in other areas. For instance, you might have accomplishments that indicate effective performance but are not stated as goals or objectives for the current year— awards, published articles, conference presentations, or election to an office in a professional association. None of these may have been predicted in the initial goal-setting process, but they are all indicative of professional success and deserve to be included in your portfolio.

PERSONAL PROFESSIONAL DEVELOPMENT

In addition to career planning and performance appraisals, the third use of portfolios by principals and other administrators is in the area of personal professional development. This is one area in which the kinds of things included and the purposes underlying the portfolio's preparation will differ, depending on your career stage—professional development concerns for someone just beginning as an administrator are very different from someone with many years of administrative experience. And though there are some clear structural overlaps with portfolios used for performance appraisal, the professional development portfolio is a much more personal document that might be read by only a relatively small number of people. It is a private collection, controlled solely by the person who prepares it; others may examine it only by invitation. Its components might include the following:

1. Platform statement. The major difference between this platform statement and those mentioned earlier is that here it is presented to help you become familiar with your own values, not to explain them to outside reviewers.
2. Goal statements. These are the goals to be sought in both the near and distant futures. They may be goals directly related to career advancement ("to complete work on my doctorate by the end of this year") or goals of a more personal nature ("to spend more time at home with my children"). They may be concrete ("to learn to use X software on my computer") or somewhat vague ("to become a better leader, particularly in conflict management"). The critical issue is that the goals should be personal, not merely statements designed to demonstrate fitness as a school administrator.

   Indicate some of your personal goals that you hope to achieve during the coming year:

   _____

   _____

   _____

   _____

   _____

3. Personal reflection. Rather than providing evidence of goals met as in the performance appraisal portfolio, this section has a more difficult task: requiring you to assess your own performance and attainment of goals. People tend to be their own harshest critics, and this is where you can write down your thoughts about what you have accomplished. This should enable you to develop a more complete view of your performance without necessarily becoming too self-critical.

   What have been some of your most impressive accomplishments, both personally and professionally, during the past year?

   _____

   _____

   _____

   _____

   _____

4. Artifacts. The goal here is not to impress another person, but to remind yourself of key events and activities related to attaining your personal and professional goals.

What are some of the things you might include as artifacts in this section of a professional development portfolio?

_____

_____

_____

_____

_____

THE POINT OF PORTFOLIOS

Although each of the three types of portfolios has been described in terms of possible contents, there is no need to adhere strictly to these lists when you develop your own material. For example, you might prefer to develop a comprehensive performance appraisal by combining two or three sections into a unified statement. You need to indicate your personal strengths. The whole point of a portfolio is, after all, to promote greater individualization of your professional development. The true value of the document lies within the material, not in what is on the surface.

Simply stated, what does a person reading a portfolio know about you as the person who prepared the document? Is there a clear picture of what the district will get if it employs you? Or will the reviewers look at the portfolio and discover a lot of form without much substance?

Portfolios are used in a variety of ways to guide the ongoing development of educational leaders. In districts where peer coaching or mentoring programs are readily available for administrators, developing a portfolio can be the glue that brings you together with a mentor on a consistent and focused basis. In addition, school districts can use portfolios as a productive method of assessing administrative performance. Although portfolios should not be relied on as the absolute summative evaluation technique, they can serve as the basis for more effective formative feedback.

Finally, using portfolios as the centerpiece of administrative professional development emphasizes the importance of individuals taking control of their own professional growth, development, and career planning. And by annually preparing and presenting a portfolio, whether to colleagues or to yourself, you can increase pride in your professional accomplishments while leaving room for further growth and learning.

CHAPTER SUMMARY

This chapter described the use of personal and professional portfolios as a valuable tool to assist you in your professional development. Not only was it noted that portfolios may be an important way for you to market your leadership skills as an applicant for administrative positions, but this technique also has other useful applications. For one thing, portfolios may serve as the basis for annual performance appraisals. Also, the portfolio can guide you in your overall and continuing professional development as a school leader. In short, the portfolio is a much more valuable tool than simply a collection of paper that can be used to try to impress potential employers.

CHAPTER 6

Presentation Skills: Effective Résumés

Maria Ornelas was known as one of the best teachers in the Forest Grove Local Schools. Although she had been teaching only seven years, she had already received the Teacher of the Year award for Abraham Lincoln Middle School two years ago. This past year, she had been the runner-up for the district's Outstanding Secondary School Teacher award. In addition to these honors, Maria was known as someone who was particularly well organized and was a leader among her peers. It was not surprising that, for the past two years, she had been pursuing a master's degree and state certification in secondary school administration at the local branch campus of the state university.

Now, Maria had finished her classes, received her certifications, and was ready to start looking for her first job as a school administrator, either here in Forest Grove or, preferably, in a school system near her hometown in the eastern part of the state. One of the first things she was asked to do by the placement office in the College of Education at the state university was to prepare an up-to-date résumé that would serve as the basis of her placement file. Maria had never had to do this before: when she had gotten her job at Abraham Lincoln Middle School, it required no serious preparation. After all, it was the school in which she had done her student teaching, and she had applied to no other district. She now had to develop a skill never required of her during the past seven years of her professional life.

Maria Ornelas is not very different from many other educators stepping into the world of job hunting as an administrative candidate for the first time. She has met the requirements of her state for the proper "hunting license," and she has had a successful prior career in the classroom. Above all, she wants to be in a leadership role of some type, and her colleagues have endorsed that goal by encouraging her in pursuing an advanced degree, certification, and now searching for a job. At this point, the "product" is ready, but the "customers" need to know about what talents Maria has.

This chapter is devoted to one of the more critical aspects of marketing and selling your leadership talents to a school system seeking administrators. Whether or not a specific school district asks you for a copy of a recent résumé, it is essential that you have on hand a brief statement of your readiness to step in as an assistant principal, principal, or some other type of administrator.

WHAT IS A RÉSUMÉ?

Quite literally, a résumé is a summary of your work life and accomplishments. It is meant to be a kind of verbal snapshot showing the highlights of your professional life. It is a quick way for employers to learn whether or not you have met the basic requirements for a job. On a different plane, however, the résumé is much more. It not only tells readers that you meet basic requirements for an opening; it can also be part of your proactive marketing of your skills, abilities, and talents. Like the portfolio described in the previous chapter, however, it is not meant to be a bludgeon used to hit reviewers over the head.

There are certain items that are always included in a résumé. Among these are:

- Name
- Addresses (both home and work)
- Phone numbers (home, work, and fax)
- E-mail addresses (home and work)
- Educational background
- Relevant work experience
- References

In addition to these basic items, you may or may not wish to include such things as:

- Significant honors, awards, or achievements
- Certification and licenses held
- Career goals and objectives

A few additional comments are in order with regard to the issue of references who will be listed in your résumé. This is an important issue, although it is rare for people to receive job offers solely because of positive recommendations from references. On the other hand, there are many cases in which people lose (or at least do not receive offers for) jobs because of bad or negative comments made by references. As a result, carefully select those who will speak on your behalf. Also, keep in mind a few additional items associated with this important part of your résumé:

- Include only people who you know will give you positive reviews. Do not take any risks.
- Contact people in advance and ask for permission to include them on your list of references.
- Make certain that the people you list as references for a specific job will actually be available if or when the school or district calls them. For example, do not include someone who will be on leave or going on an extended vacation during the spring or summer when you are applying for jobs.
- Choose only people who know you well enough to be able to speak about you completely, from firsthand information. Professors you had in graduate school might be good references, but remember that they must know you well enough to say more than simply, "Ms. Jones was enrolled in my class last semester and she received an A."
- Choose people with good reputations of their own. For example, do not include your current superintendent if he or she has recently been employed in several different school districts in your state for very brief periods of time; you never know what "baggage" the person may have accumulated in terms of reputation. Do include principals and assistant principals who know you because you have worked with them effectively as a colleague, but avoid the temptation to include people who are well known but who do not really know you. Getting "damned with faint praise" can be as damaging to you as a negative recommendation.

ELEMENTS OF EFFECTIVE RÉSUMÉS

Regardless of the items you wish to include in your personal summary, some qualities must always be present. The key ingredients in any résumé are brevity, focus, and above all, honesty.

Brevity

When an administrative position is available in a school district, it is unlikely that you will be the only applicant. Depending on the nature of the position, the reputation of the school district, the desirability of the location, and many other factors, there may be only a few people who apply, or there may be dozens or even hundreds of applicants. The trick in preparing an effective résumé is to make certain that it gets noticed and gets read, even in a sea of others. In order to do this, you must keep two things in mind.

First, an effective résumé cannot be extremely long. As district personnel administrators wade through the application materials for administrative jobs, they are inclined to seek succinct statements rather than massive collections of paper. Their primary goal is to determine whether an applicant meets the minimal standards for a particular opening. That is one reason why you need to review carefully the announcements for any openings. If a district notes that it is looking only for people with at least five years of teaching (or administrative experience), the fact that you meet that standard must be evident in your résumé. If a background in special education is either a requirement or a desired characteristic, you must also make certain to highlight that fact if it is part of your background. Do you have a master's degree if that is a requirement for the job? Do you meet the requirements of the state's education agency for an administrative credential? Make certain that your résumé clearly reflects these features so that reviewers can notice them quickly.

Review the résumé in figure 6.1 to see a sample that is clearly too long.

Notice how the person has added a great deal of information about personal goals, special awards, unrelated experiences, and a lot of other details that detract from the purpose of the résumé: to provide a brief introduction to an applicant so that the reviewers will want to learn more. How does stating a generic goal of becoming an effective principal add to the application when it can be assumed that that is the primary goal of anyone applying for the advertised administrative job? Simply adding a lot of additional verbiage does not make this person's goals any clearer. Also, note that the applicant has included such details about his personal background as "All-State Percussion Section member." Other than the fact that, as a principal, the applicant will relate well to the marching band, how does it show that the person will be an effective principal if selected for the job?

Résumé

Name: David Evans
Address: 444 Slanthill Pike
Overton, Missitucky 00112
Phones: (555) 122-7887 (Home); (555) 555-1000 (Work); (555) 111-1001 (Cell)

CAREER GOAL: To demonstrate the use of God-given skills for working effectively with children and other people in order to instill in them the true love of learning that I have possessed all through my life. I wish to be the servant leader of all who work in a secondary school and be a most effective principal who challenges all to be what they can be.

EDUCATIONAL BACKGROUND:

Graduate, Centerville High School, 1988
Captain of the football team; voted "Most Likely to Succeed in 1988"; delegate to the state committee on Athletes in Action; band member; voted best marcher, 1987; All-State Percussion Section member; co-president, French Club; selected as King of the Junior Prom; Leader of Leaders Committee; numerous scholarship offers for football and music; graduated in top 20 percent of the senior class.

B.A., State University, 1992
Major: Physical Education, Secondary Education
Played intramural football, joined the jazz band, went to Mexico twice during spring break, received the prestigious Best Dormitory Resident award as a sophomore.

M.A., State University, 1996
Major: School Administration
Received a commendation from the State University Department of Education as one of the ten most effective administrative interns in 1996.

EMPLOYMENT BACKGROUND:

1985–88, Stock clerk, Colby Pharmacy, Silverton (part-time)
1988, Lifeguard, Silverton Swimming Pool
1989, Telephone solicitor, Jefferson Paper Products
1990–92, Part-time bartender at The Watering Hole (voted the favorite after-work entertainment center in Celery County)
1992–present, Physical Education teacher, Centerville High School

I have been responsible for conducting classes in Physical Education for students in Grades 9 through 12. Among specific activities, my students have learned the use of rules and regulations related to playing basketball, volleyball, and softball. I served as a member of the schoolwide instructional improvement committee for one year and was a paid consultant to the district curriculum committee in the area of physical education for two years. In 1995, I filled in for the school principal on three occasions when he was called to important meetings downstate at the Principals' Association.

REFERENCES:

David Holdaline, football coach, Centerville
Dwayne Smith, professor of educational administration, State University
Frank Jones, Principal, Centerville High School

Figure 6.1: *An Ineffective Résumé*

In contrast to the figure 6.1 résumé, look at the much more compact statement found in figure 6.2.

In this second résumé, note that the applicant has included only information that is directly related to the job. There is contact information (address, phone numbers) and information about relevant professional experience and academic degrees earned. The second feature to keep in mind for an effective résumé is that it should be appealing to a reader. In fact, it should stand out from other papers that might be stacked on a reviewer's desk. Do not clutter your résumé with too many words or with special borders. And although the array of type fonts and sizes available these days through the miracle of word processing may be tempting to try, always remember that what you are preparing is a statement of professional interest and competence. Readers want to know about your potential ability to lead a school, not use creative

---

Résumé
David Evans
444 Slanthill Pike
Overton, Missitucky 00112
Phone: 555-122-7887

CAREER GOAL: To serve as an assistant principal of a secondary school to learn the job of a high school principal; my long-term career objective is to become a school district superintendent.

EDUCATIONAL BACKGROUND:
M.A., 1996, School Administration
B.A., 1992, Physical Education, Secondary Education

EMPLOYMENT BACKGROUND:
1992–present: Physical Education teacher, Centerville High School

AWARDS AND HONORS:
State University, One of the Top Ten Administrative Interns, 1996

ADDITIONAL EXPERIENCE:
Centerville High School Instructional Improvement Committee
Centerville School District Curriculum Committee
Assisted Centerville High School Principal throughout the year, 1999–2000

REFERENCES:
Mr. Frank Jones, Principal, Centerville High School
Dr. Dwayne Smith, professor of educational administration, State University
Ms. Agnes Cudahy, Assistant Superintendent for Curriculum, Centerville School District

---

Figure 6.2: *A More Effective Résumé*

graphics. In short, more white space on your résumé is better than too much clutter.

One last comment on the issue of brevity: there is a long-held belief that no résumé should ever be more than one page in length, but that is not always a reasonable goal or practice. The length of your résumé will depend largely on what you have done in your career. Make certain to include whatever facts about your background are appropriate and relevant for the job being sought.

Focus

The second important feature of an effective résumé is that it must be a focused representation of who you are. In other words, it should be tailored to the job for which you are applying right now. For example, if you are a science teacher and you are now applying for the job of assistant principal in a high school that is designated as a "science/math magnet school," your teaching background is much more relevant than it might be in another application. If the school where you want to work is a religion-affiliated school, your having been a student in a similar type of school as a child may be a determining factor for those selecting the next administrator. So, too, might be the work you have done as a church volunteer.

Can you have different résumés for different jobs? Absolutely. As you will probably be storing your résumés on computer disks, it is not beyond the imagination to have a separate, *more focused* statement available for nearly every job of interest. It may seem to some extent to be a contradiction to tout the importance of having a brief, tightly constructed résumé on one hand but to also note that relevant material tailored to the specific features of each job is also important, but again, the operating principle here is that your résumé must be a document that grabs interest and sets your application apart from the dozens (or even hundreds) of other applications that will appear in the personnel office.

Focus in a résumé means adding what is relevant. But it also means discarding material that does not build your case. For example, your being a teacher who has also worked on several local political campaigns may be a very satisfying thing for you, but is it truly likely to convince a reviewer that, if you become the next principal of his or her school, you will be totally committed and *focused* on providing leadership in the school?

Take a look at any two or three job descriptions in which you have had, or likely will have, some interest. If you were to apply for each of the positions, what are three or four features about your particular background that make it appear as if there is a strong fit between who you are and what they want?

_____

_____

_____

_____

_____

Honesty

It should not be necessary to mention to educators who are applying for leadership roles that, perhaps more than any other characteristic, a résumé must be honest. "Padding" résumés may help people's egos, but adding an honor here, a degree there, and perhaps a committee membership that never really happened is not only unethical, but also downright foolish. Imagine the surprise you might experience at a job interview if your résumé carries a line about how you are a doctoral candidate at a university, and you discover that your interviewer took the same single doctoral-level class that you did. However, he or she actually continued to pursue the degree through the same program from which you dropped out five years ago. Can it happen? Yes. Has it happened in real life? Unfortunately, yes. And distance from your current job and hometown is not a guarantee that someone will not discover truths that you try to hide. Networks are quite strong, and all it may take is a single e-mail or telephone call to an interviewer's friend in your former school system, university, community club, or whatever to discover that you were not really a doctoral candidate, the runner-up in the teacher of the year contest, or a major player in the Rotary Club.

To be quite candid, prestigious awards, past titles, or other glorious accomplishments are simply not the facts that close the deal in selecting people for jobs. You will (or will not) become the next principal at the Elm Street School because you are (or are not) qualified for the position, you interview well, and you fit the needs of the community. Stretching the truth on a résumé is risky business, a lie, and simply counterproductive. It is wrong and a bad practice.

Remember, too, that if this is your first application for a school administrative position, people will know that you are coming without a

lot of formal experience. You are really selling potential, not past accomplishment. Therefore, your résumé should not be constructed to make it appear as if you have experience that you do not. If you have been a classroom teacher for the past seven years, say so. You were not a "leader in instructional practices." In short, honesty can also be defined as avoiding the temptation to glorify what you think are rather mundane experiences. Readers of your application will not be fooled. Let them see an honest and open person as their potential principal or assistant principal.

One additional comment is worth stating about the importance of presenting yourself honestly. A lie told in an interview or on a résumé simply takes on a life of its own sometimes. People talk to other people who might be selecting administrators in another district—even in a different part of your state, or across the country. If you spin a story in one location and nobody discovers the untruth, you may need to repeat the same story over and over again. At some point, someone will discover that your service as the "teacher in charge of the school" on many occasions consisted of three times when the principal asked you to field phone calls during your prep period one year.

Be honest when you develop your brief, focused résumé!

ADDITIONAL THOUGHTS ON RÉSUMÉS

In addition to the discussions in this chapter about the qualities of an effective résumé, there are still some additional considerations about this job-searching and personal marketing tool:

1. Neatness counts. This is an age when visual appeal for products is critical to promote sales. No one is suggesting, though, that your résumé should include your photo, maps of where you have worked, bright colors, or clever cartoons! On the contrary, remember that the field of education is generally a very conservative one; pictures are out and white paper is in. Selling your skills as a leader of a school might be a somewhat more subtle process than trying to persuade buyers to purchase a new car. However, the lessons learned from commercial advertising are still important. What catches the eye also captures the imagination.

   Visual advertising is meant to convey a prevailing message in a product. If an airline wants to sell worry-free vacations, it shows relaxed people sitting on a beach in a beautiful, faraway destination. In contrast, the *Wall Street Journal* wants to convey a conservative image, so the layout and appearance of that newspaper has not changed significantly for many years. It offers straight, black-on-white news coverage with no colored photos, designs, or anything else to distract the reader from learning about national news, stock market reports, and international news of relevance to the business community.

2. Often, the less said the better. Often, the things that are not said are the most powerful. That is quite true in the world of preparing effective résumés. Here are a few things that many people suggest should never be included in a résumé or any other document that people may review without your control. Note that, in general, the advice here is to avoid too much personal information that is not terribly relevant to your ability to lead. Do not include such things as:

- Date of birth or age. By law, employers cannot discriminate against job applicants based on age. That being said, you cannot be sure that some reviewers of a résumé may prefer a thirty-year-old applicant for an assistant principalship over a fifty-five-year-old candidate. Is your age a factor in your ability to serve as an effective administrator? If it is not, why advertise that part of your life?
- Social security number. Once upon a time, people regularly added this piece of personal information on all sorts of documents, from résumés to job applications to driver's licenses. But with today's technology everything from soup to nuts to vacation trips to houses can be purchased over the phone or online, often with little more than a customer's social security number as a reference point. Don't give away a piece of identification that can be abused so readily.
- Indications of your religious preferences. Again, it is against the law to discriminate against job applicants based on religion. However, there are some communities where Catholics, Muslims, Jews, Protestants, or any other believers of specific religions are not ordinarily welcome. Illegal? Probably. Unethical? Most likely. Realistic? Unfortunately, in some places, this is still an issue. You may choose to rethink even applying to a place where you know this to be a concern. But if you do apply

(or in case you don't know whether religion is a concern in a given community), you can take steps to reduce the potential for negative reviews by not mentioning community activities done with a church group.

- Marital status. Some might argue that for a school administrator to work effectively with students, he or she must have children of his or her own. Or, that as school administrators must be role models for their teachers and students, they should have well-established commitments to family values. The problem with these and similar observations is that they are not based on any solid research into these matters. More importantly, determining this information about candidates during the interview or application process and then using these kinds of issues to make employment decisions is against the law. On the other hand, if you volunteer information about your personal life, people can and probably will be influenced by it.

What are some additional items that you have seen included on a résumé that you believe would be better left off the page?

_____

_____

_____

_____

_____

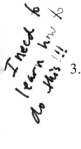

3. Learn how to brag about yourself. Most people have been told throughout their lives that it is not proper to brag. But when you are trying to land a job, you are competing with many others who are striving for the same goal. Why would a district look more favorably upon you than on all of the other candidates? One important reason is that you are bringing some special skills and abilities that others do not possess. And, of course, the only way for the employing school or district to know about your special abilities is for you to tell them. In your résumé, you must be able to point out any specific ways in which you are exceptionally well qualified for the job being advertised, and that may involve some bragging and personal horn-tooting. But again, retain your commitment to the principles of brevity, focus, and honesty. One simple statement that you were selected for an important leadership program in your community or that you were the runner-up in the district's Teacher of the Year program last year tells readers quite

a bit, even more than lengthy lists of well-known references (who may or may not really know you), and a lengthy description in your cover letter of how much this job would mean to you.

CHAPTER SUMMARY

This chapter included several tips for constructing an effective résumé that will help you in your job searching and self-marketing. The résumé is an important tool for people to get to know you on paper. It is a door-opening mechanism that may help you significantly in getting invited for an interview. Another benefit of a well-written and thoughtful résumé is that it is a written record that can be kept on file. School districts tend to have long memories regarding people who might fit in someday in the future; you might not get a job right now, but if people keep a positive image of you in their memories, you may get a call when the next position opens up.

Among the many observations made about the characteristics of effective résumés was the observation that, above all, these written statements must be consistent with three important features: they must be brief, focused, and honest.

CHAPTER 7

Presentation Skills: Interviewing

Frank Vasquez was really frustrated. He had just learned that he was no longer being considered as a candidate for the principalship of the West Loop Elementary School. Instead, three other assistant principals had made the "short list" that was forwarded to Dr. Anita Goldfarb, superintendent of schools. She would meet with each finalist and select someone to recommend to the board of education at its next meeting.

Frank knew two of the finalists quite well. The third was an "outsider" who came from a school district in the northern part of the state. All three individuals had less experience as assistants than Frank, who had spent more than nine years as an assistant principal at three different schools. This was quite bothersome to him, as he knew he had spent quite a bit of time in his interview with the campus selection team to specify all that he had done as an assistant principal in the district. In addition, Frank knew that everyone in the district was aware that he had a lot of insights into what was working in schools and what was not. One thing that people understood about Frank Vasquez was that he was not timid; he could always be counted on to express his opinions—a fact made clear during the group interview last week.

This was really getting to be quite aggravating. Frank had been in this same position five other times since getting his first assistant principalship. All he could see now was that politics were doing him in, and he was not at all happy!

Frank Vasquez is not the only person who has applied for an administrative position for which he believed he was well qualified, only to find that someone else was getting the job. Understandably, he is upset that he has tried repeatedly to achieve a goal, but with no success.

There is little more frustrating than being denied a job that you really want and that you believe you are capable of performing. After all, you have prepared for the day when you can step into a new role. You have taken courses; read books; learned techniques from mentors out in the field; and acquired the kind of insights, knowledge, and skills needed to succeed as a school leader. You apply for positions and receive word that you have made it successfully through the first round of "paper screening." You meet the stated job requirements. Now your references are contacted as the employing school district caries out background checks. Not surprisingly, you receive rave reviews from the people you have listed as references. You are invited in for an interview with a screening committee who will then recommend a slate of finalists to be considered by the superintendent before he or she offers a name to the school board for final approval.

The problem is that you never seem to be able to get to that final one-to-one conversation with the superintendent. You know that you could now be a principal if you could just get to the stage where you could talk to the real power!

Although there may be many reasons why people do not get to the next level in the search process, part of the problem that may be facing you or others in the same position as Frank Vasquez is related to the initial screening process. All of the other elements of your personal marketing plan might be in place, but the interview for an administrative position is the place where it all comes together.

Most school districts hire new principals and assistant principals after applicants have met certain prerequisite qualifications. For example, you need not apply without at least five years of teaching experience, completion of a master's degree in education, and fulfillment of all requirements for a state administrative certificate or license. In addition, some districts will only consider people with at least a few years of previous building-level experience for a principalship. Often, meeting these standards will make it likely that you will be invited for an interview of some sort. Some schools convene committees of teachers, classified staff, parents, and in some cases, students. In other cases, there may be a district-level interview team including teachers, staff, and other administrators from the district. In some settings the initial interview may be the only interview, conducted between only the applicant and the superintendent. Regardless of local practice, you will not be selected as a school principal without having engaged in some sort of an interview. Regardless of all the other work you may have put into your effort to effectively market your skills as a leader, the interview is a critical moment in anyone's pursuit of a job.

In this chapter, you will receive several suggestions to help you when you are asked to visit with one person or a whole room full of panelists.

INTERVIEWING TIPS

Regardless of the specific situation in which you find yourself as you go through the application and interview process, several predictable issues are going to come up. The following list will help you in preparing for these predictable events:

1. Anticipate "sure thing" questions. Would it surprise you to discover that among the first questions asked of you will be simply "Why do you want to be a principal?" Perhaps the version you hear will be more directly focused on the local situation: "Why do you want to work in this school, or in this district?" You can no doubt expect to hear these and several other predictable questions whenever or wherever you apply for an administrative position. You may wish to think of some other anticipated "automatic" items and write them on the lines that follow.

_____

_____

_____

_____

_____

Now, for each of these predictable questions, write out some possible answers that you can use in most interviews.

_____

_____

_____

_____

_____

When you actually get to the interview, of course, be careful not to make it appear too rehearsed, although most employers would expect that you have done some rehearsing to get ready for the interview. And do not make it appear as if you have memorized a script. Your response to each question, whether you have already prepared a response or not, must be clear, concise, free of educational jargon, and believable to everyone who hears you.

Review the list of the interview questions included in appendix B and identify those that you believe you will hear at virtually every interview.

2. Listen to the questions carefully, and respond to them. Even when you are being asked "sure thing" questions, it is critical that you pay complete attention to the person asking the question. No matter what the issue, you must act as if the person asking and the issue being raised are things that you are considering for the first time. It will not surprise people terribly that you have already thought through the reasons for wanting to be a principal, but the people asking you that question are doing so for the first time. You may have heard that same question one hundred times before, but no one in the interview room has ever heard your response before. As a result, respect the question and the person asking it. Listen carefully and respond thoughtfully. Listen not only to the words being asked, but also the way in which the question is being asked. Look for nonverbal clues. For example, does the person asking the question inadvertently smile at others around the table while asking you something? Are signals being passed to indicate, "Let's see how this one answers this item?" Remember that the members of the interview team are investing their time in you. Respond accordingly.

If you have already had some experience with interviewing for an administrative position, note any examples of times when the "how" of questions that were asked appeared to be more important than the "what" that was asked.

_____

_____

_____

_____

_____

A common mistake on the part of people being interviewed is that they answer questions well, but unfortunately, the answers are not directed at the questions asked. For example, some candidates, when asked about their strategies for increasing parental involvement in schools, leap at that question as an opportunity to

good point

expound upon their views regarding the problems with disintegrating family values, limitations on the juvenile court system, sexism in public education, the problems with single parent homes, or gun control. Although opinions expressed in this forum may represent absolutely stunning and fascinating views, they do not answer the question being asked by the interviewer: how do you get parents to show up at school?

3. Do your homework. There may be nothing more damaging to an applicant than appearing as if he or she knows nothing about the school, district, or community in which he or she wants a job. Imagine a candidate who explains in great detail how he or she would go about working with staff to improve students' standardized test scores next year, and imagine the embarrassment when a member of the interview team points out that the school just received an award from the district or the state department of education for having some of the highest standardized test scores in the region or the state! Getting profiles of the school in which you may serve as the next principal, talking to parents and other community members, walking around the neighborhood in which your prospective new school is located, and simply asking for additional information from the central office about the school are important things to do, and should be done well before the time when you sit at a table of interviewers and are asked questions about the school. (For more about this topic, refer to chapter 2.)

What are some of the ways you can learn about the school or district in which you wish to serve as an administrator?

_____

_____

_____

_____

_____

The suggestions provided in this book might not appear relevant if you are seeking a position within your own district. You might believe that you already know a lot about the particular school where you want to work. But unless you reside in the community served by the school or you have recently worked there as a teacher or in some other capacity, you probably do not know what is going on as well as you might believe that you do. Often, even if a school is in the district in which you work, you are still an outsider, and information about the school where you want to go is often the product of gossip, rumors, and other sources that cannot always be fully believed.

If it appears that you are unprepared in your first encounter with people from your prospective new school, the impression will last that this is the way that you always do business. And, as you were told many times when you first became a teacher, if you do not know an answer, say so. Then go do additional research to find out what people wanted to know. Bluffing rarely works!

4. Show passion and enthusiasm. There are several reasons for this suggestion. First, the interview committee is likely to be tired, particularly if you are the tenth candidate out of twelve to go through the process. Or perhaps you are the first person they will meet. In either case, do your best to keep all persons in the interview process fully engaged and interested in what you have to say. Although you are not there to serve as an entertainer, you cannot drone on in a monotone about some educational practice, using jargon, without putting at least part of your audience to sleep. Also, be careful to avoid being a name dropper. For example, beginning the interview with a story such as "I remember when Jane So-and-So was the principal here, when she used to tell me . . ." Jane might have been truly beloved by some, but she could have also been disliked by others—including some of the people on your interview team. Besides, Jane is not trying to get her old job back now; people want to know why *you* should be handed the keys to the building.

Second and perhaps even more important, people are looking at you as the possible next assistant principal or principal of their school. They want somebody who they think really wants the job. And they want a person who can speak with personal conviction about matters of consequence. Simply saying dryly that you firmly believe that all students can learn says very little, as contrasted with saying the same words with some degree of passion and evidence that the words are truly meaningful to you personally.

Reread your personal educational platform, as described and developed in chapter 1. Identify two or three critical ideas that you stated in that document as personally being so important that they are nonnegotiable values to you. These are the kinds of things that people will remember about you long after the interview process is completed. What are some of your core values?

_____

_____

_____

_____

_____

A third reason for being enthusiastic during your interview is that your performance at this stage gives people in the room some sense of what you will be like if you get the job as their new school leader. A key responsibility of any school administrator is being out in the community quite a bit, in front of parents, the central office, the media, and a wide range of people who need to hear about the school. In short, you need to come across as a person with enough fire to convince people in the room that you can, under certain circumstances, be a cheerleader and a good external speaker on behalf of your school.

5. Anticipate the closing question "Do you have any questions for us?" A frequent response to this question is simply a halfhearted and hurried "Gee, no, I can't think of anything right now, but if I do, I'll call you." That is generally followed by a quick departure out the same door through which you entered. It is amazing how often people appear unprepared for one of the most common closing lines used in job interviews.

As was true with the first suggestion offered in this chapter, if you know that a question is likely to come your way, why can't you prepare for it and have a ready response? This may be the last thing that a selection committee sees of you and the last words that they hear and, as a result, this might be your last chance to sell yourself effectively to a group.

List some of the questions that you might like to ask the interviewers if you are invited to do so.

_____

_____

_____

_____

_____

Remember that a final question along the lines of "When will you make your decision?" does little to reinforce your image as the potential new leader of the school. Perhaps a more powerful "closing" might be something along the lines of "From the perspectives of all of you in this room, what are the first two or three things that we should work on together when you invite me to serve as your principal?" And then listen. Make eye contact with people when they begin to talk. Do not interrupt, make any comments, fidget, or indicate that this was a scripted question. Take notes. When committee members ask you questions, they are doing so because they are intent on hearing your answers. Return the favor at this point in the interview. And also use the time wisely to learn about some of the things that you will need to deal with if you do get the call inviting you to be the next principal.

6. Practice. Practice. Practice. There is nothing to be gained from looking unprepared for an important interview. Get ready for this critical part of your job search. Go through some mock interviews if you possibly can. Ask friends, colleagues, or even members of your family to ask you questions about the job you are pursuing. Make use of the sample interview questions in appendix B of this book. The more you get to talk in practice about the issues raised in an interview, the more confident you will be about doing it for real. Most people stumble over the same questions frequently. As you go through practice interview sessions, write down some of the items that "catch" you.

_____

_____

_____

_____

   If possible, record yourself on videotape while you practice answering questions and then watch the tape. Do you talk in a monotone? Do you look around during the interview to make sure that you are making eye contact with those who ask questions? Do you have any annoying mannerisms? How do you sound? No matter how well you are prepared for the interview and no matter what you say, if the audience falls asleep or becomes antagonized because of *how* you say things, does not like you because you do not look them in the eye, or gets distracted, you will not succeed.

   If you have been videotaped in practice interview sessions, take a few minutes to write down some of the things that you did well during the sessions. Then, list the things that would bother you if you were a member of the interview team watching this applicant.

(Strengths)

_____

_____

_____

_____

_____

(Weaknesses)

_____

_____

_____

_____

_____

MORE INTERVIEWING TIPS

In addition to the basic steps in this chapter, there are some additional tips to consider as you get ready for the selection interview:

1. Arrive on time for the interview. It is almost silly to mention this, but it is unforgivable to arrive late for an interview. Besides being rude and thoughtless, you are also giving decision makers an unfavorable impression of the way in which you may conduct business if you get the job.
2. Walk into the room confidently. Remember that people are looking at you as a potential leader in their school. On the other hand, be careful not to walk in like a gunfighter from a bad movie. People can quickly tell the difference between confidence and arrogance.
3. Shake hands with everyone in the room. Of course, this depends on a few important variables like the size of the room and how easy it is to get around the table where interviewers are located. And it also depends on the number of people who are present. Shaking hands is a good idea, but it should not be done in an awkward or uneasy fashion.
4. Jot down names of people as they introduce themselves. Make a kind of "seating chart" as people introduce themselves around the table. Note how they introduce themselves and, when responding to them later, use the same title that each person used during the introduction. Also, if you know someone in the room according

to one name socially ("Pete") but he introduces himself as "Dr. Jones" in the interview setting, be careful to use the formal title during the interview.

5. Begin by thanking everyone for his or her time and interest. Remember that this has been a long day for those sitting around the table—even if you are the first person to be called in.

6. Avoid negatives. Above all, never say anything bad about present or past employers. You may be working in a horrible situation now, but no matter what the reality is, people in the room who are thinking about bringing you to their school or district can only wonder if you will say negative things about them if you look for another job someday.

CHAPTER SUMMARY

This chapter provided several tips to help you be more successful during the interview process. Whether you are interviewing for a position in a school or district where you know everyone or have worked with many of the people who are involved with the selection process, or you are seeking a post in a district where you are a complete unknown, treat the interview as an important tool for getting the job. While you are "on stage" in the interview setting, you have the ultimate opportunity to underscore your overall marketing strategy by selling yourself and closing the deal. Keep in mind that you want to be honest during this phase of the selection process, but you also want to make people realize that you are the best person for the job. In fact, even if you are not selected, you should be trying to make certain that the selection committee will regret that you were not the one selected because you came across so well during the interview—whether the interview was very short or very long.

Nothing offered in the chapter is presented as a magical or sure way to get the exact job that you want. But if you take time to consider the tips shared with you here, and if you practice and think about what you are going to do during an interview, you are likely to get to the next step more frequently than you may have in the past.

CHAPTER 8

Recap and Reflection

It was one of those occurrences that happen so often in schools. Two teachers at Ravenswood Elementary School, Lorenza Garcia and Anne Whitman, had both recently completed the coursework required to complete their principal certifications at Glen Este University. Anne had started her program, taken a year off when she was transferred to Ravenswood, and completed her program during the same term as Lorenza had, even though Ms. Garcia had started her graduate work about a year later than Anne. But the two had shared many experiences at the university. For example, they had both "survived" Dr. Silas's statistics course, and they had often carpooled as they raced across town after school on afternoons when they both had to attend 4:30 classes at the university. Their common university studies had brought them together as colleague teachers at Ravenswood, and they had become close friends as the years of common work had progressed. Both were about the same age, and both had families. Lorenza had two children ages five and nine, and Anne had three at home: twin eight-year-old boys and a girl of three. And both teachers had the respect of the other teachers, counselors, and administrators at Ravenswood. In fact, Joe Ellington, their principal, had even made a joke about the even quality of his two teachers after he had written letters of recommendation for both to add to their placement files at Glen Este. "I probably should have saved a lot of time by just making photocopies when I wrote about the two of them. They're both such great teachers, and I really believe that Anne and Lorenza are ready to step in and make a difference as assistant principals in this district or some other system that is looking for strong educational leaders."

It was now late May, and the two friends were chatting in the Ravenswood teachers' lounge. The topic of conversation was the recent job searches that they had gone through. They had agreed at the beginning of this school year to provide support to one another as they applied for jobs as assistant principals in local schools. They knew that they might often end up as direct competitors for the same jobs, but they had promised to retain their personal friendship.

The most intense period of job applications had begun in mid-March. Since then, Lorenza had applied to nine schools in the county, and Anne had forwarded her applications to six. They overlapped at four schools, and in three of those cases they had both made it to the final interview stage with the superintendent. Throughout these experiences, the two maintained their pledge of friendship and had several meetings to review their experiences with each other. Today's session, however, was quite a bit different. Anne was celebrating the fact that she had gotten a phone call last night inviting her to sign a contract as an assistant principal at Ralph Waldo Emerson School in the Lake City School District. It was a great job with an outstanding beginning salary, good fringe benefits, and the opportunity to work with a terrific principal, Steve Diaz, an administrator generally recognized as one of the most innovative and effective principals in the state. But she was restrained in her enthusiasm because she knew that her friend and colleague had been the other finalist for Emerson. Lorenza was unsuccessful again, but this time she had "lost" to someone she knew. Today's conversation was painful. "Anne, I am so pleased for you, but I have to be honest with you. I really thought that I interviewed well at Lake City. We have so much in common that I know that we look like twins on paper. But I still lost. I'm really getting discouraged. After nine attempts, I still can't get a job. I think I'm about ready to throw in the towel."

Lorenza's comments may sound quite familiar. You may have gone through several applications for administrative jobs recently but may have always come up "empty." And each time that you did not get selected, it seemed to hurt a little more. Your confidence, self-esteem, and enthusiasm have no doubt taken a beating. And your story may parallel this scenario in that you have watched friends and colleagues achieve the success that you are seeking. So what's happening here?

Throughout this book, numerous observations and suggestions have been offered to help you achieve success as you seek an administrative position. This advice is offered regardless of whether you are now just beginning to seek your first job as a leader or you have a number of years of experience as an educational leader and you are now seeking a new challenge.

This concluding chapter offers some closing thoughts and reflections about the process of seeking administrative positions in schools. Each is offered as advice or a tip that you may wish to recall in the future. The preceding chapters have presented ideas related to helping you market your leadership talents and then present yourself effectively to potential clients or customers. Here, the emphasis is on pulling the earlier ideas together to assist you, whether you have been successful in closing the deal or not.

TIPS FOR REFINING THE SEARCH

Unless you are incredibly fortunate as a beginner, you are not likely to get a job offer from the first school or district to which you apply. In all probability, it may take several unsuccessful applications before you even make it to the semifinals or finals and get the interview that enables you to sell your skill at the powerful one-to-one level. There are likely to be many applications that receive no response at all until you finally get a final letter of rejection that begins with a statement such as "Thank you for your interest in the administrative opening in our school district. There were many very talented and capable individuals who applied, and our decision making was exceptionally difficult. Unfortunately . . ." After a while, you will be able to develop almost a sixth sense about the contents of such letters without even opening the envelopes. In other cases, you may not even receive a formal letter of rejection. Instead, you may hear through the grapevine that the job at X school was filled, and thus you learn that you are no longer a candidate.

Regardless of the process that may be followed in any specific case, try to do something that you have probably told your students many times during your career as a teacher: "Keep learning from all that you do. There is no such thing as a failure." In this regard, a few suggestions are in order to help you:

1. If possible, get feedback. This suggestion may be difficult to follow these days, largely because employers are often quite fearful of follow-up litigation filed by unsuccessful job applicants. "Say nothing and protect yourself" seems to be a common motto and piece of advice offered to any employer who must reject apparently qualified (at least on paper) applicants

for a job. The wisdom here seems to be that if you tell people why they did not get a job, that can be held against you at some point in the future. As a result, a view of "the less said the better" has been adopted by fearful personnel managers in many organizations.

Regardless of these observations, it is still recommended that you seek feedback about your applications whenever possible. In many cases in which you do get a response, you may hear endless lists of platitudes such as "it was really a coin toss among several outstanding candidates," or "we were so fortunate—kind of like kids in a candy store. You shouldn't feel as if you lost. You simply were not the winner we decided to select." On the other hand, you may actually get some useful feedback from time to time from someone who truly wishes to help you as a colleague. For example, you may learn that your résumé was too long, or that the school was looking for someone with a few more years of teaching experience. Perhaps the tiebreaker between you and other candidates was a lack of experience on your part in working with special-needs populations. If those are the kinds of things that you hear, you can improve your future job prospects by staying in the classroom another year or two, cutting down on the wonderful things that you say about yourself in your résumé, or working to gain more insights about students with special needs.

2. Avoid quick rationalizations. A temptation of many people, after finding out that another candidate got a desired job, is to rationalize the selection in terms of racial, gender, ethnic, linguistic, or some other preferences on the part of the employer. This is a soothing and simple approach that might make you feel better at first, but it may also cause you to begin to ignore real issues. "I didn't get that job because they were really only looking for a Hispanic (or African American, or Asian, or whatever else you may wish to imagine) woman, and I'm not one." Such a statement may make you feel better, and, to be honest, it may very well be accurate. But dwelling on this type of thing does nothing for you in the long run; there is nothing you can do to change your race or ethnicity or your gender, or to acquire instant fluency in a new language overnight. If you continue to explain events in terms based on perceptions of unfairness and bias by others, you are more likely to end up feeling like a victim than a job applicant. If you are a man, and a woman gets the job you want, remember that

the district may have wanted a female administrator who was as good or better than any male applicant for the same job. Live with that fact and accept the decision.

Also, adopting the view that you did not get a job because "they were looking for women, or African Americans, or Hispanics" will do little to help you develop the positive attitude and outlook that will be apparent during interviews and eventually help you get the position that you really want. People who constantly blame others and blame politics often stay in their original positions for a very long time.

3. Keep talking to others. As the two teachers in the opening scenario discovered, the opportunity to keep talking to friends—even friends competing for the same positions—can be extremely beneficial. You may not have a situation quite like the one described featuring Anne and Lorenza. It is stretching reality a bit to think that you will work in the same school, share similar backgrounds, and then apply for the same jobs as a teacher across the hall from you. But it is important to have a friend to whom you can turn and talk with periodically. In some cases, it may be an administrator who has worked with you or encouraged you in your career. Or it could be another teacher in your school or your district. Or it could be a family member. Knowing someone who can listen to you when you need to vent frustration or celebrate successes is very important. You also need someone who knows you well enough to give you straight, honest feedback every once in a while; this feedback can help you significantly not only in landing a first job, but also in performing more effectively when you finally get the job you are seeking.

TIPS FOR REBOUNDING AND IMPROVING

When most people were little children, their parents often told them the importance of getting right back up after they fell down. That same advice continues to be important throughout people's lives and careers. Here are a few suggestions to assist you in getting right back up when you need to keep going:

1. Avoid the "I give up" syndrome. As Lorenza felt in this chapter's opening scenario, there are likely to be many days when you feel

as though your decision to go into school administration was just about the dumbest thing you ever tried. You worry that you will never succeed in even getting a job, let alone being effective. Just remember that there are many reasons why people are sometimes not selected for one thing or another. Like everything else in this world, there are never going to be absolute guarantees that you will always get the perfect job. At the same time, remember that landing a good position is always a matter of simply getting the right call at the right time.

2. Don't blame others, and don't blame yourself. There are many reasons why certain people are selected for jobs. There are also many reasons why some people do not get jobs. It is no one's fault if you do not get selected, even if you have not been selected many times. Too often, people begin to blame the employing school districts, their boards of education, the superintendents, the local politicians, their professors in graduate school, and virtually everyone else who happens to be around. Or they begin to blame themselves.

Consider the example of one young woman who was unsuccessful in several job interviews. She began to notice that, when women were chosen for the jobs she wanted, they tended to appear older and more serious. Before her next interview, she changed her hairstyle to make her look quite a bit older, selected very conservative clothing, and began to wear eyeglasses instead of her normal contact lenses. Each change was meant to change an overall image that the woman thought made her appear too young and not enough like a principal. None of these superficial changes helped. Your appearance, educational background, and other personal features are not the issues that will necessarily get you a desired job. If you are in this trap now, remember that blaming others after not being selected for a job will not help you achieve your goal, which is to get picked after your *next* application. Looking backward all the time does not help you as a driver, and the same can be said about your efforts as a job applicant.

3. Don't worry about "hidden agendas." One of the reactions that people have after not being selected for a job is to assume that the choice was driven by politics. That may often be the case. After all, you may be an excellent candidate, but you are not the person that the superintendent needs to place in a particular school because he or she needs someone who knows the issues currently

facing a particularly volatile local community. And so, a person "inside the system" is picked instead of you or instead of some other person who might seem exceptionally well qualified. Live with it. It is a decision based on politics, but it is a reality of life in most organizations, especially public schools.

4. Reflect on what has happened. Instead of blaming others, yourself, politics, or even the alignment of the planets in the solar system, the answer to any frustrating question is often the most obvious one. Think about what you have done to succeed—or not. In one recent case, a frustrated candidate who did not get a desired job confided to others that the only reason he did not get the job was because of politics. He did not recognize that, during the interview for a principalship, he repeatedly tried to convince the panel of his case by citing all of his experience as an assistant principal for several years. He failed to recognize that his arguments were not effective because his focus clearly should have been on his future plans as a principal for the school.

NEXT STEPS

If you have followed the advice in this book and achieved the career goal that you have desired, congratulations! However, your job is far from over. Now, your focus must be on following through with the explicit and implicit promises made during the application process. Too often, job applicants treat the selection process as a type of game, in which winning is defined as getting a job. Actually, getting the job is the easy part because it is only the beginning. Good luck with the next part!

If, however, you have not been the person selected for a job, keep trying. There are many excellent, well-qualified, and experienced principals who have been trying to step into new positions for years, but they have not yet been successful. They keep trying.

If you are currently a teacher who wants to be a school administrator, here are a few additional tips to help you achieve your goals:

1. While waiting, keep doing the same excellent job in the classroom that you have done for years. For one thing, your students deserve nothing less. Also, you will continue to demonstrate to everyone around you your sincere commitment to your duty as a

professional educator. This is the kind of thing that any school or district will prize on the part of future and prospective leaders.

2. Keep up to date. Although you may have gotten an A in school law four years ago when you completed your master's or certification program, remember that law is a field that is constantly changing. So are finance, computer technology, and virtually everything else in which you may have been exposed to ideas just a short time ago. Continue to read professional journals and to participate in inservice programs sponsored by local, state, and national professional associations. You might also wish to take more university courses. Stay current!

3. Network. Talk to others about your goals. Keep in contact with former professors, principals, fellow students from graduate schools, and all others who can lend a hand in telling you about job openings, new trends, and so forth.

4. Reread your educational platform periodically. Looking over the document you prepared to help you "Know the Product" in chapter 1 has at least two continuing benefits. First, you can revise it if your attitudes or dispositions change. In fact, they probably will. Second, even if you have not changed, reading your platform from time to time will be a way for you to recall some important aspects of your value system that may be critical during a future job search and application.

5. Begin building a leadership presence. There is no question that you are a leader in your classroom, but you are not yet an administrator. It is critical that, while you await your opportunity to land an administrative position, people around you get to know your skill as a leader who can work effectively with students, staff, community groups, parents, and others with whom principals and assistants work each day. Participate in campus improvement work. Serve on committees. Do whatever you can to heighten your profile as a potential administrator.

As an aspiring school administrator, what are some additional things that you plan to do to help yourself in marketing your leadership skills and talents?

_____

_____

_____

_____

_____

If you are now an assistant principal and you want to become a principal, here are a few suggestions to help you make the most out of your current administrative position:

1. Remember your role. You are a school administrator, to be sure. You have worked hard and made many sacrifices to leave your familiar role as a teacher and become an administrator. However, you are not in the same inner circle as your principal. You may no longer be a teacher, but when meetings are held for administrators in the district, you are often the one who has to stay at school and take care of business while the principal is gone. But if you have a long-term goal of becoming a principal, you must use your time to cultivate skills you can use when you have your own school.

2. Cool your ego. Assistant principals get some of the worst and dirtiest duties of administration. You deal with a lot of complaints and conflict with students, parents, community members, and staff. While you do these things, your principal probably gets the credit for most of the good things that happen in the school. You must avoid the temptation to feel like a victim or feel sorry for yourself. Remember that you are an assistant principal and not a coprincipal. You were not hired to be the lead administrator; your job is to assist the lead administrator. Most likely, you were hired because you appeared to have the potential to add your skills to what was already present in your school. You were probably selected because people assumed that you could work effectively with the principal and supplement his or her talents. Make yourself appeal to others seeking to hire you as a principal by reining in your pride and ego.

3. Assist the principal. Never forget that your job is to assist the principal. One of the most important ways to provide that support is by making the principal look good and achieve success. You must learn to suppress your desire to call attention to your own activities and accomplishments. Your job is to remain in the shadows and do what you can do to make your school effective. By accomplishing that objective, you will appear to others as an administrator in a highly effective school, and that will be quite appealing to those seeking a new principal for their schools.

4. Practice discretion. No one is likely to hire a principal who goes around airing dirty laundry about his or her school to the public. Do not get into the habit of making critical comments about your

boss—the principal—in public. Whether you are blessed to work with a great principal or forced to work with someone less capable, remember that you owe your boss loyalty and discretion. You may be tempted in conversations with teachers, other administrators, parents, or community members to criticize your principal's work, but remember that if others hear you speaking ill of someone, they will wonder what you are likely to say about them in their absence.

5. Listen, listen, then listen some more. The great advantage of keeping your mouth shut and cooling your ego is that you are likely to learn a lot of things very quickly. You will share a very simple learning technique with hundreds of students: listen and absorb. Be careful about getting involved in situations in which you react to issues by making absolute, unyielding, and rash decisions. Those who are likely to consider you as a principal at some point in the future may find a candidate who never backs down—right or wrong—to be anyone but the kind of person ready to lead a school.

6. Ask to do more. Assistant principals often get typecast in their roles rather quickly. If you have been the assistant principal in charge of little but attendance and discipline for several years, you will not be an appealing candidate for a school searching for someone who knows a lot about curriculum and instruction. It is essential, therefore, that you develop skills and expertise in many areas of campus management while serving as an assistant. If you are the only assistant in a school, it may be easier to gain experience in a wide range of areas. On the other hand, if you are part of a larger team of assistant principals and your colleagues have already been assigned specific areas of coverage, you may need to find alternative ways to learn about the full range of functional activity in any school. To do this, talk with your principal from time to time about gaining additional experience. Most principals will not be terribly surprised to discover that one of their assistant principals wants to move up in administration.

7. Stay alive professionally. Despite the many limitations on your time and energy as you serve as a very busy assistant principal, you need to find ways of staying in tune with important developments in education. Not doing so will make it quite difficult to persuade a school or district that you are ready to serve as a principal of your own building. There are two recommended areas in which you

should pursue further professional growth while you strive to sharpen your leadership skills. One is reading, and the other is participating in professional seminars, meetings, and conferences.

8. Stay positive. This last recommendation may be the most powerful one because it touches on all other items listed. Be as enthusiastic and positive as you can about yourself, your job, your colleagues, your students, and your school district. Although this is not always easy, a positive attitude will be a strong signal to others that you have the ability to manage the frequent frustrations and stresses that accompany the position of school principal. Always remember that you are "on stage" throughout your career, and that someone is likely to be watching you and judging your potential as a school leader when you least expect it.

As an assistant principal, what are some other strategies that you have tried or will try in the future to keep refining your ability and your marketability as a future principal?

_____

_____

_____

_____

_____

CHAPTER SUMMARY

This chapter offered some advice to those who have not yet been able to land the administrative position for which they may have been searching. Suggestions were given to assist you in rethinking many aspects of your current behavior and activities in school and to signal to outsiders that you may indeed be the one who can be an effective leader in a particular school. Remember, once again, that those selecting you for a principalship, assistant principalship, superintendency, or any other position have very high expectations for their new school leader. You cannot ignore that trust and the hopes of those who may hire you. Returning to the analogy of business marketing suggested throughout this book, it will always be an extremely difficult task to close the deal if you cannot suggest to potential clients that you know yourself; you care about them; and you have the knowledge, skills, abilities, and positive disposition to benefit their schools. People have high hopes for you!

Excerpts from Educational Platforms

The following are examples of recently developed platforms by school leaders across the country. Note that none of the statements follow a precise format. Also, you would likely find significant changes in some aspects of these platforms if you reviewed them in the future, as all of the educators represented here have engaged in periodic revisions of their views.

EXAMPLE 1

What is my view of the purpose of schooling?
The purpose of schooling is to teach life skills, both academic and social.

What is the appropriate role for teachers?
Teachers should provide structure and learning opportunities. They should be mentors and consultants, and not foster the idea that they are the students' primary sources of knowledge and information. In fact, they should emphasize to students that being articulate, having appropriate social skills, and being problem solvers are far more important than all of the facts they will ever learn.

What do I want this school to become?
This is the tough part—having a vision of what I want my school to become. A principal can have all the credentials in the world, but without vision it may all be for nothing more than mediocrity. I want my school to inspire a sense of security, warmth, and capability that is based on substance, not fluff. I want everyone associated with our schools to be happy and proud. How this will be done is not my call. It will be decided jointly with staff, faculty, and parents based on their suggestions, initiatives, and

hard work. I believe that the principal should provide the compass, not the road map.

How do I want others to see me?

The image that I wish to project to others would not change just because I became a principal. I want people to see me as capable and caring, a person just like them, a person doing his best to ensure that the children in my building are being properly educated. I want them to view me as approachable, someone who is willing to listen and help them, and as an honorable person whom anyone can trust under any circumstances.

What are my nonnegotiable values?

On this one, it's tempting to give a politically correct answer that does not honestly reflect my feelings about this issue. Truthfully, although I feel that I have high values, I would think long and hard before becoming involved in a confrontation that would force my resignation. It seems to me that another employer might not wish to hire someone who has left a former district under a cloud, regardless of the reason. I can only think of three circumstances under which working for a particular employer would be intolerable—if the activity endangered others, if it was illegal, or if it required me to be dishonest. Except for these three things, I would probably do my best to continue working with or for others who might be violating my personal values.

EXAMPLE 2

View of Students

The role of education today has significantly changed from just a few years ago. As society has changed, the demands of education have changed. I believe that it is our duty as educators to give students the necessary skills to survive—and not only just to survive, but also to lead successful lives. In order to do this, I believe students need to have basic knowledge: reading, writing, and mathematics. But along with that, students must be able to be independent thinkers. I believe we must give them the tools, skills, and strategies necessary to solve problems as individuals and as members of a team.

Personal Expectations

I have high expectations of myself and of others around me. I try to surround myself with people who have a positive outlook on life. I do not have time to listen to those people who say, "It can't be done." I prefer the phrase "What can I do to help?" I am very service-oriented and care about children's education and well-being. I hope that I am portrayed as a motivator for students' success, as an enthusiastic person, and as one who is not afraid to work.

Role as an Administrator

I believe that communication is extremely important. I want to be an effective communicator through listening and observation. Many things can be accomplished through effective communication.

I believe there must be mutual respect in all types of relationships throughout the campus.

I want to provide teachers with a school climate in which they feel they have the opportunity to have shared decision making. I want to provide a school climate that allows for trust to learn and grow. A climate in which teachers feel that they have a right to voice opinions and concerns. One in which everybody knows the end goal and everyone is working toward it.

As administrator, I know that I must take the role of a visionary and I must be able to visualize how all the separate parts can come together to benefit the whole. But I must also see my role as the person who takes care of the details of the day-to-day life and activities necessary for teacher success. I must follow through with things that have been promised to teachers, so that they may have the trust in me to know that they can depend on me to lead them.

I realize that I am in the early stages of my role as an administrator. I know that I have much to learn and realize that there is much experience to be had. This is the view of my role as I begin the road to leadership, looking to never stop learning and growing.

EXAMPLE 3

The Role of the Principal in Learner-Centered Leadership

In order to have a successful learning environment it is the goal of this administrator to create a safe atmosphere of trust, openness, friendliness, and mutual respect. This atmosphere will facilitate learning by allowing the entire school community, which includes students, parents, faculty, and staff, to share their resources and ideas. It is also my goal to empower the school community to take risks that will enhance the educational experience, not only for the present but also for the future.

The Role of the Principal in Facilities Management

The administrator's role in facilities management is extremely important to the atmosphere of the school. The grounds are the first thing that the school community and the public see when entering or passing by the school. It is important that the grounds are kept clean and safe for the perception and impression of the school to be a positive one. All members of the school community must take ownership in the facilities where they work and learn. It is my goal to ensure an ongoing maintenance program of the grounds and building, not only to include custodial staff but also to include every individual within the school community. By taking ownership in the school and school grounds, we will instill community pride and make the institution an inviting place to be. Utility costs can be extremely high; therefore, conservation will be an important issue within the facility and can also be used as an educational tool for the betterment of our environment.

Personal Vision Statement
The entire school community—which includes faculty, staff, students, and parents—will be empowered to achieve success in learning. The school community will provide a morally safe and healthy environment and will be an engaging and exciting place to learn with a diverse set of peers. I believe that the school community will attain success when we work, care, learn, and grow together.

EXAMPLE 4

Purpose of Education and Schools
Schools are to develop the whole child. The school should focus on providing the child with knowledge, building character and morals, fostering physical development, and fostering social development.

Role of Students
Students must develop a level of responsibility that is commensurate with that of their age-level peers. They must become active participants in their education and must confer with teachers and other students about the educational content and process by which they are learning.

Definition of Curriculum
In our district, the curriculum is what the state mandates for each child to be taught and evaluated on. The district has a committee that chooses the textbooks. The local campus is able to identify its own specific needs and then teach the curriculum to all students.

EXAMPLE 5

Student Achievement
Student achievement may be assessed in different ways. Mastery of academic skills is certainly important in education today. I have learned that

a carefully planned curriculum can guide a teacher because it addresses critical skills and organizes the different concepts needed. Yet I also believe that growth and success can be evidenced by behavior and not just test scores.

EXAMPLE 6

I believe that all children can learn and should have the opportunity to do so. To not impart knowledge and understanding to our students is to jeopardize our own future. And although the learning type is dependent on many factors, it is our responsibility as educators to do whatever is necessary for our children to function in society. In our constantly changing society, we must prepare the entire child for the future academically, socially, and emotionally.

* Children come to school from as many backgrounds as there are children. No longer can we use the cliché "one size fits all." I believe we must develop a child's academic skills on an individual basis. We must challenge students with interesting, relevant curricula and materials that will serve them long into the future.
* Teachers act in the place of parents during the school day. Therefore, it is important that morals and values become an integral part of a child's education. Children must be taught to do the right thing, and we must become proactive with children's social development.
* Our children are emotionally fragile and must be handled with the utmost care. As educators, we must be able to have patience and teach patience, have empathy and teach empathy, be understanding and teach understanding. Our students' emotional well-being must be a priority in our educational system.

I believe we must focus on what is best for our students. Each of our students should be treated with respect and dignity, with our decisions being made as if the students were our own sons and daughters.

I think an instructional leader must clearly communicate expectations. An instructional leader will take risks, since this is how success is often measured. I feel that a strong instructional leader will develop and keep good teachers, supportive parents, and successful students.

Sample Interview Questions

The following questions have been collected from principal or assistant principal interviews at several school districts across the nation. Although variations on many of these can be found in different districts, these will give you some sense of what may be asked of you. Some are fairly common, but a few are not likely to be asked in too many settings. Regardless of what questions you look at, practice answering them with a colleague who can detect whether or not you are actually addressing the question. One of the remarks often made by interviewers is "Candidate X did a great job of answering. Unfortunately he or she did not answer the questions that we asked!"

1. From a principal's perspective, what does it mean to monitor the educational program of a school? How do you do it in a way that is acceptable to your staff?
2. What does the word *integrity* mean to you, and how does integrity manifest itself as you carry out your professional responsibilities?
3. Time is a scarce resource. How do you manage time to ensure that you are a peak performer?
4. If you visited a school and determined that site-based decision making was alive and well, how would you know it?
5. We are concerned about developing a nurturing, challenging, and disciplined environment in our schools. What specific things do you like to see happen in a school in order for that to occur?
6. What evidence would lead you to believe that a parent organization is effective?
7. What do we need to do to empower staff to be truly effective agents for change? Where does the principal fit into that picture?

8. Describe in the clearest detail possible your vision of what a truly effective (elementary/middle/high) school would look like.
9. What teaching methods do you find bother you a great deal?
10. What do you enjoy about listening to people?
11. Describe a situation that you handled recently that required great sensitivity and tact.
12. How do you define self-esteem, and how do you build and enhance self-esteem in your staff?
13. What are norms, and how might they be used to enhance decision making at the school site?
14. Describe how you would lead a meeting in which you know that all participants have had numerous heated arguments and disagreements about the central topic of the meeting.
15. Describe one person you most admire, and say why you admire that person.
16. What words would your best friend use to describe you?
17. What words would someone who disliked you use to describe you?
18. What variables in a school often stifle peak performance in its staff?
19. We often hear descriptions of "centralized ends and decentralized means." What does that term mean to you?
20. What do the concepts of *quality*, *equality*, and *equity* mean to you? What have you done in the past to enhance each concept in schools?
21. How do you feel about the evaluation of staff, and what do you feel must be done in order for the process to be mutually beneficial?
22. If you were to ask someone to facilitate a group process in your building, what specific qualities would you look for in the person you chose?
23. How do we develop an atmosphere of high expectations for self and others?
24. Is everything we do in education that adds value to a child's education measurable and/or observable? What are the exceptions, if any?
25. If you were hiring a new secretary, what questions would you ask applicants for the position? Why?
26. Are we trying to do too much or too little in education? If so, what should we abandon or add?

27. As a principal, what is your current role in the development and implementation of curriculum in the school?

28. Someone once said, "Go slow so you can go fast." What is your reaction to that statement?

29. What is it like to take a risk in a school? How do you feel about risk taking on the part of yourself and your staff?

30. Describe something that you have tried and have failed at. What did you learn from that experience?

31. What motivates you personally and professionally?

32. There is a growing concern that we are using only a small part of our collective potential in schools. What operational essentials must be in place if we are to maximize our collective potential?

33. Why is visioning so important personally and professionally?

34. If you could take a year off and write a book, what would the title of your book be and what would be the essence of the message you would want to convey to the reader?

35. What was the last book on education that you read?

36. What was the last book that you read?

37. If you were to go to your last school a month after you left and asked the staff what your legacy had been, what would they say?

38. Describe a recent professional conflict you had and indicate how it was resolved.

39. How would you delegate responsibilities to other administrators and staff members to ensure the success of the many activities in the school?

40. What qualities would you look for when hiring new teachers on your campus?

41. Describe how you would encourage the participation and involvement of parents in your school.

42. What would be the role and expectations of the counseling program, particularly in the area of student discipline?

43. How would you work with a site-based school improvement team to develop an effective school plan, including a strong evaluation component to measure success?

44. Describe the process that you would use to develop a campus budget.

45. As the new principal on a campus, what leadership skills would you use to build your team from existing staff?

46. Describe a creative, original, innovative idea that you have implemented in your school.
47. What are two or three significant issues facing educators in our state, and how do you plan to address these if you become our principal?
48. What are your hobbies?
49. When was the last time you had a really good laugh, and why?
50. Why do you want to be a principal (assistant principal)?

Add any other questions that you have heard as you have interviewed for positions as a school administrator. Make special note of any questions that you hope no one will ask you during an interview. Then prepare answers to those questions.

_____

_____

_____

_____

_____

About the Author

John C. Daresh is currently a professor of educational leadership at the University of Texas at El Paso. Prior to that, he held faculty or administrative positions at the University of Cincinnati, Ohio State University, and University of Northern Colorado. Daresh began his career in education working in high schools in Dubuque, Iowa, and in the Chicago public schools. For most of his academic career, his scholarly work has been directed toward high school improvement or professional development opportunities for school administrators. He has served as a speaker or consultant across North America and in England, Holland, Lithuania, Israel, Taiwan, and South Africa. Daresh has published more than one hundred times on these subjects in research and practitioners' journals, and has written or cowritten ten books in addition to the one you are now reading.